THE SONG OF THE LARK

Sister Agnes, of the diocese of Aberdeen and Orkney, was born in Nottingham and spent her early years in a small mining town, the daughter of a fitter's mate and his handicapped wife. At an early age she was influenced by the life of Francis of Assisi, and also by the more spartan spirit of the Celtic Church. An introduction to Scotland added a touch of magic. All these, and the tragic early death of a much-loved mother, drew her inevitably towards the fulfilment of the religious life. After more than twenty years as a Franciscan Sister in Devon she began a new religious life as a solitary on the remote island of Fetlar in Shetland. She has now been joined by other Sisters to form a new community.

Also by Sister Agnes
A TIDE THAT SINGS

With line drawings by the author

SISTER AGNES, SOLI

The Song
of the Lark

TRIANGLE

To my friend Rosemary, with loving thanks.

First published 1992
Triangle
SPCK
Holy Trinity Church
Marylebone Road
London NW1 4DU

Second impression 1995

British Library Cataloguing in Publication Data
A catalogue record for this book is available from the British Library.
ISBN 0-281-04624-7

Typeset by Inforum, Rowlands Castle, Hants
Printed in Great Britain by
BPC Paperbacks Ltd
a member of
The British Printing Company Ltd

Contents

Acknowledgements

Again I am deeply indebted to Mrs Dorothy Jamieson for her encouragement and constructive criticism.

Also, to Simon and Joan Potts for the gift of a word processor and to Kevin King and Nick Baisley for helping me out of the Dark Ages through their instructions how to use it.

Lastly, though not least, my thanks to SOLI, for taking on much extra work so as to enable me time to write. Thank you . . .

Foreword

Born and brought up in the traditions of the Presbyterian Church of Scotland I had no encounters with nuns until I went to school and first met them in the pages of Chaucer's *Canterbury Tales*. My next encounter was when studying the reign of Louis XIV, with his suppression of the Convent of Port Royal in 1709 and my last was during a visit to Salamanca in Spain, while on a pilgrimage to Santiago de Compostella. I took shelter from the noon day sun in the cool cloisters of the delightful sixteenth century Dominican Convent of the Duenas and listened to the nuns at their devotions.

It was shortly after my return from Spain that I was invited to become a Trustee of the Society of Our Lady of the Isles and therefore acquired 'my own nuns'!

'My nuns' are perhaps the newest order in the Anglican Communion. It was founded in 1989 by Statute of the Bishop of Aberdeen & Orkney, Shetland, where the order has its headquarters, being part of ancient Norse Diocese of Orkney which passed to Scotland at the time of the Impignoration of Orkney & Shetland in 1469.

Those who have been fortunate enough to read Sister Agnes' first book, telling of her decision to become a Franciscan nun and how her subsequent visits to the Scottish islands persuaded her to set up her own contemplative sisterhood, will be delighted to read this sequel, which brings the life and work of the order up to date.

Those who are also fortunate to know Sister Agnes will know of her pleasant determination, and will therefore not be surprised to learn that she has now been able to draw into the order one 'full-time' nun in the person of Sister Mary Clare, who is vividly portrayed in the book as well as the Caim Members of the order whose work, particularly in nursing in the Shetland Islands, is so much appreciated.

It is a fact of Shetland life that the Shetland Islands Council is concerned at the decline in population of Fetlar and it is therefore greatly to the credit of Sister Agnes and the Society that to some extent this decline is now being halted. The population is below one hundred and would probably have declined further and more rapidly had the Society not set up its base on the island, bringing many people from all over the world who come to visit the order. Shetlanders, who are by nature a reticent people, are now beginning to realise the benefits of having an order of nuns in their midst and are now becoming very proud of them.

Thanks to the far-sightedness of Sister Agnes and the sheer enthusiasm of Sister Mary Clare in pursuing an imaginative building programme, the order is set to expand further, which can only be to the benefit of the island of Fetlar in particular and Shetland in general.

When you come to the end of this book you will be privileged to have an insight into one of the most remarkable women in late twentieth century Scotland. Single handed she has forged a way of life which most of us would not dare consider and has done so without material resources, other than what she has been able to create. Sister Agnes is the living example that determination, combined with honest piety, can still provide a way of life which is both contemplative and active, a life which most of us would envy but which very few of us have the courage to embark upon.

Robert Chalmers
Diocese of Aberdeen and Orkney

Prologue

Every fibre in my body is stretched to the limit as I cling, knuckles white, to the sides of the passenger seat and pray that we'll make it safely. As the car swings round the last corner, the brakes squeal and we can now see from this point on the road that all cars for the Toft Inter-island Ferry have already been driven on deck. The ramp of the small boat is slowly rising into its upward position and I do believe that after all Sister's efforts to get us here, we're too late to board. No, just a moment . . . as we jerk to a halt the ferry man who's operating the ramp is glancing up at the skipper on the bridge with raised eyebrows, and now . . . yes! He's turned and pressed the button. Grinding downwards, the ramp bumps into place and thankfully we slide over it. Had we not caught this particular ferry we'd have had hours to wait at the north end of the island of Yell for the last boat to Fetlar.

'Thank you, Sister . . . Well done. I'm glad I wasn't driving.'

'Thank you, Sister Agnes, for trusting me. Are you all right?'

'Just about, let's get out for a little fresh air.'

Yes, we'd timed it neatly though not without strain. Yet I'm of the opinion that life must have some tug and pull, some elasticity, in order to attain balance.

After our mad drive we lean on the rail of the vessel and over the swell of a calm winter sea watch the treeless hills of the Shetland Mainland recede into a blur of greys and blue. Ahead, the hills of Yell are already rising into focus, dotted with the occasional croft house. In all their varying moods I've delighted in these beloved isles surrounded by sky and ocean: glassy-calm, tempest-tossed, happy, wild, free, yet always beautiful to the heart that loves them.

Sister and I have no need of words during moments of shared joy such as this scene brings us. For this kind of experience is carried in the soul and speaks an eternal language of its own. It is voiced today in both of us, in an utterance of 'We're en route for Home . . .', an inexpressibly beautiful 'route' to the place that we love.

Once on the island of Yell we're a step nearer our own hearth. We'll soon be winding our way through its peaty landscape the seventeen miles or so north to the Gutcher ferry, where we should, with a few moments to spare, catch the boat for Fetlar.

Several days away from home are usually enough for those of us who live as a small religious family on one of the most northerly isles of Shetland. This time we'd torn ourselves away from Fetlar in order to see a friend off on her long journey back to New Zealand. Now we await her return later in the year, when she's to join our ranks.

Many people, like Pat, have come to our isle since I first wrote about my life as a solitary here in the north. Some of them were only in transit, never to return, whilst others flock to us again and again and, like the elements around us, in varying moods. A few have infiltrated into the heart of my life, and it is these who have been woven into the fabric of this sequel – a story which tells of the loving generosity of God; a story which, like life, begins where it ends, and ends where it begins – on a pilgrimage home.

As a solitary I found great happiness and great love. Yet who can be entirely solitary who's united with God? Where there's life there's love, and where there's love there must be another to whom one can give that love. For me, that 'Other' is God, a God who gives back a hundredfold and who gives Himself in and through so many things and so many people.

In my life now, God comes to me most especially through the religious family He's given me, and among whom there's much scope for give and take, for one and another, for ebb and flow, for black and white and all the colours of the rainbow. Thirty years ago I gave Him a life that longed for love and he gave me Himself. Out of that has burgeoned forth wholeness, joy and that for which I asked – that melody which is my song – the song of the lark.

Lark, skylark, spilling your rubbed and round
Pebbles of sound in air's still lake,
Whose widening circles fill the noon; yet none
Is known so small beside the sun.

Be strong your fervent soaring, your skyward air!
Tremble there a nerve of song!
Float up there where voice and wing are one,
A singing star, a note of light![1]

'I know,' I said to Sister Mary Clare as we pulled up outside
The Ness several hours later and caught sight of the dimpsy
outline of the first of our new buildings out on the headland,
'let's call our new home, when we manage to build it, "Larks'
Hame".'

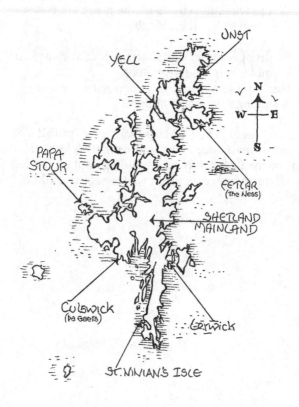

UNST

YELL

N
W   E
S

PAPA
STOUR

FETLAR
(the Ness)

SHETLAND
MAINLAND

Culswick
(Da Gaers)

Lerwick

St. NINIAN'S ISLE

1   A Distant Song

The letter flapped in the breeze, and with it a strange spurt of hope filled my heart. Steadying the pages, I looked again at the thick expansive writing. It could have been tidier, even more carefully phrased . . . It was decisive, I would give it that . . . though I had had many letters over the past few months saying exactly the same thing . . .

'Dear Sister Agnes,' it began. 'Thank you for writing your book . . . Would it be possible for me to spend some time with you on Fetlar?'

Lodging the sheets beneath a tumbler of water on the garden table at which I sat, I caused a kaleidoscope of shape and colour to emanate from the cut glass. Shafts of sunlight caught the diverging facets and life, my life, sprang into focus as an intricate design.

First, the brilliant colour of a gloriously happy childhood given to my sister and me by our poor, though richly loving parents. Followed by the dark lines of our mother's death, plunging the pattern suddenly into the twists and turns of a long period of spiritual growth in a convent in Devon. Years later, came the shining visit to Iona where a tiny shoot of a seemingly impossible call broke the surface, only to be blanketed by a few more years of darkness. Until, joy, out of the darkness exploded light, the light of a life lived on a remote northerly isle in Shetland where, in this place, peace took root, a peace which in time burgeoned into the deep dimensions and fullness of the solitary vocation.

Thoughtfully, I picked up the letter and reread it. Was it as special, or as providential, as it seemed? Was God, in fact, about to shake the pattern of my life on Fetlar into a new formation? Was this woman, Mary, a schoolteacher working in Worcester, to add a new kind of lustre to it? Only time would tell. Slipping the letter back into its envelope I pushed it into the deepest pocket of my habit, collected up the two or three pieces of crockery on a tray, and carried them into the tiny porch/kitchen to wash them up.

My mind slid this way and that. Besides Mary, hundreds of new contacts had come my way through an invitation to write my story two years previously. It had happened like this:

After spending my first few years on the island without anything in the way of a break, my friend Rosemary began to press me to take a holiday, arguing so convincingly that I started to save. Penny by penny, enough money was laid aside, so that after a period of time I dutifully made plans to go south, intending to visit my sister Carole and two other friends.

Rosemary herself had kindly started the fund, which eventually made possible not the intended relaxing break, but a busman's holiday – a holiday which lasted for three long weeks. During those weeks, whilst travelling through Scotland and around England, I talked, answered questions and even preached. The two churches in which I was asked to preach were, to my amusement, situated at the extreme ends of Britain – the first, the Church of the Deaf in Aberdeen and the second, St Levan's church in Cornwall, close to Land's End. Interestingly, it was during this somewhat strenuous tour that many people suggested that I write down some of the things that I had told them.

So it was that, the day after my return from this so-called rest, whilst sweeping down the stairs at The Ness, I found myself considering the real possibility of writing my story. In a kind of way I was discussing it with the Lord, as I brushed up the dust and heard myself telling him that it would give me great pleasure to write . . . Yet would I be capable? 'You're aware, Lord,' I rattled on, 'that I've no education to speak of and it would be extremely time-consuming, wouldn't it? And since life isn't long enough anyway . . . Yet, yes, I'd really enjoy to try my hand with a pen.' By the time I reached the bottom step, having come to no conclusion over what I suspected was, well, maybe only a dream, I decided to leave it with Him. This I did, with the result that three hours later I received a large envelope by the afternoon post from the Editor of Triangle Books. She informed me that, having read an article about me in the *Church of England Newspaper* she wondered if I had ever considered writing my story. If so, 'Would you be able to write it yourself or would you like someone else to write it for you?' There was now no doubt in my mind as to what the answer to both these questions should be. So in due course my book, *A Tide that Sings*, was written and published with the result that hundreds of new friends, like Mary, moved into my orbit.

Wiping the last knife, I decided to slip down to see Rosemary about dates – Mary's and others. There was just no point in saying yes to a whole hoard of visitors whilst she herself was away.

Four-and-a-half years earlier, Rosemary, a retired school-teacher and a great friend of mine, had insisted in her characteristically determined manner upon coming north to help me settle into The Ness. The Ness is a small croft house situated on a south-facing headland of Fetlar. As I had guessed at the time, she secretly held the view that I was mentally deranged to settle in such a bleak, end-of-the-world-sounding place. So, what was my joy when, after only a fortnight of helping me to scrub floors, emulsion walls, hang curtains and tidy up the garden, she admitted, slightly sheepishly, that she was nego-tiating to purchase the other crumbling cottage adjacent to mine.

At this point where my sequel now begins, she had settled happily into it as my friend and neighbour.

I pulled on my boots and was soon sipping a hot mug of coffee and staring thoughtfully through the window of her beautifully renovated croft house at a flock of sheep on the hillside opposite. The Ness burn, meandering along its skirts, glinted in the summer sunshine and a couple of tubby lambs leaped back and forth across a plank that spanned it.

'In a strange way,' I ruminated, 'I feel that, somehow, I ought to say yes to Mary. The problem is, that she's chosen an absolutely impossible week to come.'

'Yes, I do understand,' Rosemary murmured, 'but you

simply can't have everyone to stay who asks. I'm only sorry that I'm going to be away south, whilst you're so busy. Also, that you'll have the added labour of having Kelpie to look after.'

'Oh, he's fun, I'll enjoy him,' I assured her, 'and some of the visitors will delight in having a jolly little dog to take for a walk.'

'Good,' she smiled. 'Though if I were you, I'd suggest that this Mary comes in the spring next year, instead of now – unless, of course, you're thoroughly set on squeezing her in.'

'Mmm, well that's the thing . . . Somehow, I think I should, and actually there's just one week in September that she may be able to manage before the gales begin. If not, it'll have to be the spring.' I stood up and moved towards the door. 'I'll have to dash, Rosemary, there's a job in the garden that I simply must finish. Thanks for the coffee. I'll see you at Vespers.'

On this glorious June day I clambered over our homemade stile at the end of Rosemary's garden and on over the rough ground up to The Ness, my home for over four years. A couple of furry objects bounded to greet me; or was I wrong and was it instead to parley with me for an early tea? They were Flugga and Skerry, the two sable-coloured tabbies, who had been the dearest of companions to me since I had arrived on the isle. Right behind them, ensconced as rearguard on the garden wall and looking infinitely superior, was Mooskit, whose name in Shetland means mouse-coloured grey. Mooskit was my latest and as dearly loved acquisition – a happy mistake of a cat, or whatever one might like to call him, who, despite my impulsiveness in acquiring him only the year before, is a great darling.

My blunder over him had begun one evening when Hazel from Velzie had telephoned with a request. She wanted to know if Rosemary would be interested in a 'peerie kitlin'. Rosemary was in Devon at the time, trying to sell her Il-fracombe house with the hopes of coming north to live permanently on Fetlar. Hazel, knowing this, and knowing also that she had recently lost her elderly terrier, Tikki, thought that a kitten might be a comfort to her.

Later that evening when Rosemary rang, I tentatively introduced the subject of kittens. My friend, knowing well my weakness for cats, let alone kittens, saw at once through my flounderings. Baulked by her instantaneous and without-any-doubt-about-it reaction of 'No more kittens!' I gave up – at least for the moment. Fortunately I understood that, at this stage, it would not be the most diplomatic thing to mention that I had, in fact, arranged to see the litter the very next day.

Six weeks later Rosemary arrived home, pink with pleasure, and announced that she had a marvellous surprise to show me. 'Close your eyes, Sister Agnes,' she said as she clambered down from the cab of the furniture van. There was a whispered, 'Could you lift it down now, please, Derek?' and, 'Yes, over here please . . . Thank you . . .' Derek, our great friend and driver of the van, was obviously moving something fairly hefty, for I could hear laboured breathing, along with a thud or two and then, 'Now, you can open them, Sister . . .'

Rosemary, bending forward, unlatched the mesh door of a sizeable container. 'Right,' she waved. 'Do look,' and in a trice, out shot a squib of a dog who exploded into a frenzy of jubilant motion. 'It's Kelpie,' she cried. 'Isn't he a darling?'

'Yes, yes,' I replied, bracing myself for the next bombardment. 'Is Kelpie *your* pup?' I knew at a glance that he and Mooskit could never, ever, in the whole of their days, live under the same roof. They were far too alike.

'Yes, he's mine; you do like him don't you? I just couldn't bear the thought of being without another dog.'

I studied the small wheaten-coloured cairn for a second or two. 'Yes,' I replied, 'yes, he's perfectly lovely . . . and I*'ve* got a kitten!'

That had all happened the year before. Now, Mooskit, sleek and handsome, with four ridiculously long legs, jumped from the wall, sidled alongside me and pushed his soft, almost adult, silvery grey body against my ankles. Skerry, as 'Uncle Top Cat', stalked ahead, tail held high, quivering with the anticipation of yet another meal, while Flugga, dear Flugga, with a characteristic flip of his tail, brought up the rear.

Having satisfied the appetites of my feline family, I hurried

5

upstairs to change. At the top of the narrow stairway is a tiny landing from which one can enter a loft room on either side. Bending low, I turned left into the neuk, as we call it, which is the place in which I sleep, think, write and relax. I glanced, as I always do when entering, through the northern skylight which looks out over the vegetable patch and on up the road that winds down to The Ness. It is a good place from which to ascertain if I am likely to be entertaining a crowd of unexpected visitors at any moment, and for this reason it is very useful when I am working up there. It also means that if I do see folk coming, papers can be left undisturbed whilst I pop downstairs, put on the kettle and then, when they have arrived entertain them in the but or the ben.

Unbending myself to the central height of the room, I pulled Mary's letter from my pocket and placed it thoughtfully on the table. Through the southern skylight warm sunlight flooded in. I blinked in its dazzling rays as I changed into something more suitable for the garden and soaked up the familiar view of sky and ocean. The Out Skerries, ten miles away on the horizon, hung sharply suspended against a ridge of cloud. 'Mmm,' I thought, 'that's an ominous sign of rain, so the locals would tell me . . . Yes, I must hurry and get those cabbages into the ground as soon as I can.'

Dibbling in the last plant of 'January King' I stood, stretching my aching joints. More clouds had banked up west of the Hoga, that basking lion-shaped strip of headland which is a well-known feature of the Fetlar landscape. It would be marvellously convenient to have a shower of rain now, I decided, scanning the neat soldierly rows of greens, it would save me lugging at least a dozen buckets of water out to the plot. Flugga, who had been helping, rolled on to his back, perilously near the plants, luxuriating in the feel of the warm soil. Calling him off, I breathed in a deep whiff of the ocean, mingled with the smell of the earth. The sights and smells of God's creation and the knowledge of my part within it gave me a sublime sense of well-being, which in a contradictory way was contributed to by my stretched muscles and that gorgeous feeling of tiredness that always comes from the physical effort of hard work.

I wound in the garden line, tussling it to and fro to release it from Flugga who, springing insanely after it, then dashed head-over-heels across the garden, up over the dry stone dyke, and disappeared. After he had gone a sweet, almost tangible silence descended. Standing a moment or two I breathed it in. 'Lovely!' I sighed as, picking up the tools, I made my way over to the old closet where they were kept. Hard manual labour was, I had found, rewardingly meditative, as are so many practical, mundane jobs if done for the right reason – the right reason being always for me the glory of God. How very much, I pondered, this attitude can transform the simplest act into a means of prayer.

Whilst about my work, I had been thinking mostly of the future, for Mary's letter was still much in the forefront of my mind. Could there be something divinely meant by it? Was God perhaps sending her to be my first Sister? If so, and having waited so long for a companion, did I still feel that first, original enthusiasm that I had once had about starting a community? No one, least of all myself, could say that I was the type to found an Order and anyway, I had grown very used to being on my own. Could I, now, enjoy sharing all this space and freedom, the glory of this place and a life lived for God? Could I cope, in fact, with living so closely alongside another human being? Four years earlier I would have said a spontaneous 'yes', for I had had a vision. That vision now needed a little dusting down and taking from its shelf.

Courage had been needed to come to Fetlar, to answer what I believed was God's call to bring the religious life back to the Scottish islands. Yet, with His help, and the realisation that I had nothing to lose, with the wise and encouraging advice of Father Lewis and Rosemary's stalwart friendship, not to say her laughter, blessings had abounded.

Rosemary did not feel either the need or the challenge to join me in the sense of becoming a Sister. Instead, she had bought Lower Ness and had lived as an associate beside me, sharing the recitation of the Divine Offices, the work of the day and some of our lovely recreational hours. What joy and freedom of spirit those early days had brought – to be able at the drop of a hat to go off for a walk; to sit above the beach and watch seals and otters and every kind of rare bird; to have the time and space, just 'to be'.

In the material sense I lived from day to day with no regular income of any kind; this too, brought its freedom. I sold vegetables, though more often than not I gave them away, for they made lovely thank offerings to the friends who had been generous in giving their help to me. Only, ever, did I ask God for what I thought I really needed and there was always enough.

Almost from the moment of my arrival on the isle, friends and strangers alike had asked to come and visit, and an even greater percentage – just turned up! They came, mostly, to share something of the lifestyle and to breathe in the quiet beauty of God.

Over the years that passed, my values were jostled around and sharpened in all kinds of ways. So that, as I continued to live the religious life as a solitary, delighting in the rhythm of the Church's year, I grew to love God in a deeper and more silent way. New dimensions opened up and as one year slid into another I found, with surprise, that although many folk wanted to join me in a loose-knit sort of way, no one asked, or seemed to desire, to become a fully committed member of the hoped-for community. My original idea of a small, family-sized unit started to diminish and the seed of a question mark took root and began to grow. Maybe I had got the whole thing wrong? Maybe I was meant to go on and develop the solitary vocation instead? Now that was a thought that appealed to me! I began to hope . . . and this, of course, was when Mary wrote!

The first plop of rain landed on my nose. Hurriedly, I scraped some soil from my boots and, making my way into the house, I washed quickly, put on the kettle and changed for Vespers. Skerry and Mooskit were curled in an abandoned embrace on my bed, looking as though they were always the greatest of buddies – which they are not. What a lot of lessons they can teach us . . . Mary's letter on the table caught my eye, rain spattered the skylights, the kettle clicked itself off and I went downstairs to make a quick cup of tea.

It's now three years since I received that letter from Mary, and as I trace back over those years my heart rejoices in the blessings that the life here has brought us.

I'm lying, lazily, against a warm rock, high on the hill north of The Ness. Climbing up is more of an effort these days, for I've become plump and middle-aged. The day is almost hot, which is unusual for Shetland, and I've come to this lovely spot to think and just 'to be', for a precious half-hour or so. Also to breathe in not only the mild salty air but that special, ever present, peace, and indeed sense of the immensity of God which is always to be found here. Terns wheel around, flashing between me and the sun, their wings translucent and their voices harsh. Whimbrels strut to and fro, not fifteen yards away, whickering to their young, while a couple of irate oyster catchers have swung over the loch to fly on over the valley towards the hill of Stakkaberg. Wavelets of water tickle my toes and Tildy, our Australian terrier, has pushed her warm body into mine where she snores mildly after the climb; she, also, is middle-aged. We nestle together and I too close my eyes and relax. Tensions slide away, moments dissolve into infinity and sleep almost overtakes me.

Suddenly, I'm awake. Narrowing my eyes to a half-open slit I stare upwards, dazzled and entranced. Far above the symphony of birds, the whispering grass, the slap, slap of the water and the whole spectrum of this corner of God's creation, hovers high in the heavens a tiny speck, its song instantly known . . . It's the song of the joy which I was given as a child and in my growing years. It's the song of that gift which I asked of Christ when I gave Him my life. It's the

9

song of the hope which carried me through years of darkness and pain. It's the song of that glory which gave me a glimpse of heaven and which enables me to share what I can of its joy and fullness. It's a haunting air, the song of the heart, the song of the heart of the world . . . the heart of the universe. It's the song that has brought into being all that is . . . Or is it just simply . . . the song of a lark?

I, who sought solitude, have founded an Order. I, who sought the embrace of God, am now able to embrace others and, with them, to be enfolded by Him. In 1988 I stood at a crossroad here on Fetlar, vulnerable and longing to take the route of a hermit. I'd found a pearl of great price, or so I thought, and was afraid of losing it. This way, the solitary way, I reasoned, would ensure its safety. But God, the great Weaver of Life, had a different plan, a design of intricate beauty, mapped out not only for my life but for the lives of those who would join me. One by one He had taken each thread, each colour, and woven them into mine. The complex Celtic patterns and interweavings of my life as a solitary have remained in structure much the same, though in essence they've been illuminated by the characters and love of those who have come to join me. Nothing has been lost, only gained a hundredfold. No, I needn't have feared that my relationship with God would be diminished in the sharing, for every dimension of the past, the present and the future has been sharpened and brought into focus.

As I squeeze my eyes to peer harder into the heavens, I see the tiny flash of light still hovering . . . From it, note after note of pure joy is transmitted to my own heart. Yes, it seems to encompass all things, the whole of creation, the whole world . . . the whole essence of life in its song.

. . . The Song of Love.

2 Fledgelings

I heard my letter land with a thud at the bottom of the island postbox. Pushing in the rest of the mail I hitched my rucksack into a comfortable position on my back and tramped the mile and a half back to The Ness.

'Dear Mary,' the letter had begun, 'I'm afraid the dates in July that you asked to visit Fetlar are not possible as the only accommodation that I have is a caravan which is already booked. Could I suggest that you arrange to come in September . . .'

Her reply came almost by return of post:

'Dear Sister Agnes, Thank you for your swift reply . . . Unfortunately, I shall be working during the week of September 19th–26th . . . However I do have a week's half term from the 23rd October. Would this be convenient? . . . My friend Frances . . . would love to come too, if there is room and if, despite weather conditions the return can be guaranteed . . .'

Because of the ever-present possibility of October gales I could not of course guarantee their getting off the island at any given date, and since they were reluctant to risk the eventuality of being stranded here, there was a break in our correspondence. However, there still persisted a niggle or two in my mind about this woman Mary, and now, added to it, was Frances her friend. Strange, I mused, that one should be called Mary and the other Frances! The community that I thought to found was to be dedicated to Mary the Mother of Christ, and the spirit of it would be, in part, that of St Francis of Assisi.

A couple of weeks later I waved Rosemary off on her holiday south and at about the same time found, unexpectedly, that I had a holiday cancellation here at The Ness. The cancellation was for the original week that Mary had asked to come so, without losing any time, I sat down and wrote to her:

11

'13th July, 1988

Dear Mary,

. . . I can now offer you from the 21st–28th of this month, as a lady from Hull had to cancel her holiday due to the illness of a friend. If you are young enough, agile and adventurous enough to come up at such short notice, you and Frances would be most welcome. In which case you must give me a ring so that I can prepare . . .

   I do hope that you will come . . .
                    Yours in Christ,
                              +Agnes (Sister).'

This missive had fallen on to the doormat of the girls' boarding house where Mary worked, at the precise moment that she was stepping over it to go off on an organised Quiet Day at a local Anglican convent. Hastily she had torn open the envelope, devoured the contents and spent the rest of the day in a whirl. It was months later, when she knew me better as a real human being, that she divulged that the Quiet Day had not been such a quiet one after all. She and Frances had spent most of it trying to work out how they were going to get up to Aberdeen to board the ship for Shetland, with only four days in hand! Needless to say they managed it, and to my delight Mary gave me a quick buzz on the telephone before the ship sailed. 'We're actually on the St Clair, and about to sail,' she burbled. 'We can't believe that we're going to see you tomorrow . . .' A thrill of excitement rippled through me and I wondered why. Lots of people had stayed with me at The Ness, yet I had never experienced a feeling like this.

   The next morning, the 21st July, dawned bright, and at 10.15 a.m. I drove the old banger of a car that Rosemary and I shared, down to the Fetlar ferry terminal. The terminal, quarried out of a northern promontory of the isle, consists of a docking place and a ramp for one ferry boat only, for Fetlar has no harbour. The scene, desolate, hard and unwelcoming, gives a first-time visitor to its shores a dreary impression. Two small wooden buildings stand near the ramp. The first contains lavatories and a telephone that is usually out of order and the other is for the use of the Inter-island Ferries.

Being on the early side, I pulled the car into a passing place on the hill above the terminal. The ferry boat, still a sliver on the blue mirror of sea, gave me time to sit and stare. The two shadowy islands of Yell and Unst rose mysteriously from the ocean four or five miles away, and leaning back I enjoyed the tranquillity of the scene. Imagining the excitement of my two visitors, I felt as I always do a little shy of meeting new friends. Fulmars glided to and fro, a gannet plummeted every so often into the waters and a lark carolled above.

Ten minutes later, leaning over the handrail of the ramp I watched two or three cars drive off the vessel. Straining my eyes to see Mary and Frances I noticed a group of foot

passengers hovering around one of the ferry men and one of them, a dark, well built and attractive woman about my own age, turned and waved. There was a hold up, it seemed, about luggage, though after a moment or two one of the ladies stooped, picked up her bags and walked off the boat towards me. As she drew near I recognised her as an old friend who came occasionally to Fetlar for a holiday. I greeted her with a cheery hello, though to my surprise, neither smile nor greeting was returned. No one had ever snubbed me in this way before and I was stunned. However there was no time to lick my wounds, for Mary and Frances, beaming from ear to ear, staggered up the ramp with masses of luggage. Frances, in her late fifties, was older than Mary and shorter in stature and a much quieter person in contrast. The one threw her arms around me and the other greeted me with a smile.

'We've had a catastrophe,' they chorused. 'The ferry man, that one, over there, was painting the boat and accidentally dropped a tray of paint all over one of our bags. I looked down at a fawn holdall streaked with white paint. 'It's holding my interview kit,' grimaced Mary, and then laughed. 'It seems absolutely fated.'

'Yes,' added Frances, 'and you'll hardly believe this, but only minutes before the paint landed on it, it was trundled off the boat on to Unst.'

'Then,' said Mary, 'we had to tear like mad after it and snatch it back before sailing on here to Fetlar.'

Laughing with them I squeezed the bags into the back of the car, trying to avoid soiling the paintwork or anything that Mary's sad receptacle might touch. Then we all clambered in ourselves. 'Did you say your "interview bag"?' I questioned as we wound along the narrow road, pulling up and in and out to oblige the odd sheep cropping grass along its verges.

'Yes I did. It's all rather exciting,' Mary enlightened me. 'You see, I've been short-listed for a fabulous job back in Canada.' She flashed a knowing smile at Frances. Then, leaning over my shoulder to be heard more clearly above the rapping of the engine she went on. 'Eighteen months ago I was widowed, after living with my husband, a doctor, in Canada for seventeen years. Since we had no family I continued to work and after taking further degrees in English and psychology accepted various teaching posts.' She could have added that she became a highly qualified teacher in the field of Special Needs, though did not. She continued: 'Due to my husband's ill health we returned to Great Britain last year when sadly, soon after our arrival, he died. I was stunned, and in part I'm still reeling from the shock. Life has to go on though, and my first thoughts with regard to the future have been to return to Canada; back to the wonderful friends I made there. Meanwhile, Sister Agnes, and it's absolutely wonderful, this fabulous job opportunity's come up . . . It's for a visiting professor at New Brunswick and the interviews are to be held in London at the end of this month. I'm to be notified any moment, as to exactly when the date will be.' She paused breathlessly for a second. 'So you see, that's the reason I've brought my interview kit with me, just in case I'm still with you on Fetlar when I receive my call to go south.'

'How lovely for you,' I smiled. Secretly thinking of the splattered bag, I wondered if God had perhaps been trying to tell her something else!

Once home, I showed them the caravan that they were to share. They were enchanted by it as by the croft house, the sea views, the freedom and the fresh, unsullied air. What a lovely start this is, I thought, though I must persuade them now to come in and have lunch.

Not being a confident cook I had prepared several pre-cooked meals before my visitors arrived and poked them into a battered, second-hand freezer that stands at the back of the byre. This would give me space to feel free with them, for we could go walking and perhaps take out a picnic or two and really have time to enjoy each other. Yes, in a strange sort of way I was looking forward enormously to the following week.

It was one of the loveliest summer weeks of the year, so not only was I able to share with them something of the lifestyle that I lived but also to share something of my beloved island. Mary very kindly offered to walk Kelpie each day, for she had two dogs of her own at home and was missing them. They fed

Rosemary's ducks, enjoyed the beach and savoured every moment. I loved having both these dear women, though I must admit that I was just a fraction overawed by Mary's exuberant enthusiasm for life. I confided this to Frances one day and she smilingly replied, much to my amusement: 'Yes, Mary does talk quite a lot!'

From Mary's talk, though, I learned a great deal about her as a person, the main thing being that she was of an extremely evangelical, Church of England persuasion. Her father, a priest, had been killed in a bomb blast that had hit their home during the war. She, only a tiny baby at the time, had, with her mother, miraculously escaped death, though not without what turned out in later years to be an undetected injury to her spine. Eventually her mother had married another clergyman, a kindly man who had been a close friend of her deceased husband and who became a wonderful stepfather to Mary. He too, was a Low Churchman, so no wonder that this woman who had so wanted to come to Fetlar bombarded me with questions such as, 'What do you feel about the Virgin Mary?'

All too soon the last night of their stay arrived, and before packing up their luggage ready for the early morning start, they went off in the evening sunshine to say farewell to the few island friends they had made. Several hours later, having arrived back, they sought me out. Mary, looking deadly earnest, asked if I could possibly spare her a few moments to talk.

'Of course,' I agreed. 'Is it something important?'

'Well yes,' she started eagerly. 'You see, Frances and I had a serious discussion on our walk, the outcome of which is that I would like to make you a proposition.

'Come upstairs to the neuk,' I invited and she followed me into the house. Quickly settling ourselves into two fireside chairs in my tiny room I gently encouraged her to speak. At that time, having begun to suspect that Mary might indeed have a vocation to the religious life, I myself, strangely, was beginning to get cold feet in case it should be to Fetlar. Yet despite this, I was simply bursting with curiosity to know more of her 'proposition'. We had already had a couple of deeply interesting talks on the subject of her life with her husband in Canada, and I knew that she was searching for a deeper truth and commitment. Could it be that she was looking towards the possibility of a vocation, and that my original intuition about her had been right? Of course, I did realise that the Canadian teaching post, if she was offered it, might easily provide her with all kinds of new dimensions.

'I won't waste any time in coming to the point,' she burst out. 'I realise that life here in the summer, with Rosemary away, with unexpected visitors coming off the ferry and calling in to see you and others actually staying, is a busy one and must be tiring. So, since there's been no word about my interview, my proposition is, would it be a help if I stayed on another week, not as a guest but to help you?'

'Well . . .' I hesitated.

'Make me a work list, a timetable . . . Oh please do! I'd so like to lend a hand, and as you know I love cooking and I would happily make cups of tea all day long for as many folk as turned up.'

It sounded very tempting, yet I knew from experience that it is often easier, when one is busy, to do a job for oneself than to organise another person. As graciously as I could I declined her kind offer. At the same time, I had noticed over the past couple of days that she had dropped a hint or two, almost without realising it, that she might be drawn to my type of lifestyle. This, as I have already said, is what I had wondered when she first wrote to me, though now, having seen and watched her within my own environment, I was not so keen that it should be to Fetlar, and had become uncertain. It would be easy to misunderstand this. I liked her a lot and would have felt the same about anyone at that point. It was a feeling that if she were being called then I hoped it would be to somewhere else. Oh dear, was she beginning to turn her sights towards Fetlar? If so, and if God were calling her here as a Sister . . . was I really quite ready for it? And was I absolutely certain, and had I really made my mind up, that after four and a half years here on my own I was still meant to start a community? In a flash I saw all the precious freedoms and joys of the solitary life fleeing away . . .

For a second or so I stared thoughtfully through one of the skylights at the soft clouds sailing above. Then, turning, was jolted back into the reality of the present moment by a look of terrible disappointment on Mary's face. So much so that, meta-phorically speaking, I rapped my knuckles. Yes, why shouldn't she have a vocation? She was an extremely nice person. A bit garrulous perhaps, yet . . . Well, as far as fitting in on Fetlar went she'd be good at cooking . . . and many other things . . . Yet she had done so many other things already in the trying of this and that, and there still remained deep inside me a sneaky feeling that she just might be the kind of person who had itchy feet, and at this point in her life be running away from unhappiness. She continued to look so downcast that a great chunk of me minded horribly and felt mean.

This feeling did not dwindle as the evening lengthened and eventually I turned again to Mary's friend Frances.

'Frances, what do you feel about Mary staying on for a little longer?' I asked.

'I think that it would be absolutely wonderful of you if you could allow her another few days. She'd be a great help I'm sure . . .'

Before she could say more Mary herself appeared.

'Mary,' I said, 'I've been thinking a little more about our conversation, and if it really would give you pleasure to stay on, then please do. I'd like you to . . . and you're right, it would be a treat to have the cooking side of things taken care of.'

She looked at me in astonishment, then grinned, her face radiant. 'Thank you, Sister, I'd simply love to. Thank you – so much.'

Despite her delight at the prospect of staying on, Mary had a very disturbed night. I learned later that she had tossed and turned and turned and tossed, thinking of all the reasons why she ought perhaps to go home after all. Relatives were hoping to spend a day or two with her during the school holidays, her mother had been unwell . . .

So at the crack of dawn the next morning when I went out to help Frances load her luggage into the car, she told me that her friend had decided to leave with her after all. A strange feeling of relief flooded through me, though I smiled sympathetically at the dismal-looking Mary as she hove to with her baggage.

Twenty minutes later we were en route for the ferry, during which journey my two passengers remained unusually quiet. Until, that is, we came within view of Brough Lodge.

'Oh, please, would it be possible to pause, Sister Agnes, whilst I take the last shot in my camera?'

'Of course, Mary, we've just about time,' I responded, pressing down the foot brake and pulling sharply into the passing place which lay above Brough. 'This should make a perfect photograph for you.' Soaking up the beauty of the rising sun casting long shadows and a rosy glow across the walls of the edifice, I switched off the engine.

As Mary climbed out of the car I could not help noticing the tears she was trying to hide and, indeed, was still trying to hide ten minutes later when she and Frances waved their final farewells from the deck of the boat. The small vessel sailed into the summer haze and as it did so I saw also, somewhat to my surprise, that it was not only Mary's cheeks that were wet.

The following week was terribly busy, for folk poured off the ferry on to the isle and many of them meandered down to The Ness. Three visitors came actually to stay during this time, including a youngster whom I had taught in the Devonshire convent Sunday school seven or eight years ago. Nicola's much looked-forward-to visit gave me great joy. At this time, she was studying medicine and had especially chosen to do some of her practical training in Lerwick so that she could visit me on Fetlar. She had grown into a lovely girl and I was deeply touched that our friendship, which had begun whilst she was still a child, through a mutual love of poetry, had remained an important part of her life.

As the week gathered momentum five other people arrived. A family from Fife, they came to camp as they had over previous years, in Rosemary's garden with her ducks. They had become good friends of mine and kindly arranged this annual visit with the idea of helping me with any jobs that needed to be done. On this occasion, they started on the painting of Rosemary's caravan, something we had intended to do for some time, transforming it into a beautiful grass green colour to blend in with the landscape. They also painted my garden fence and did various repair jobs. Whilst all this hustle and bustle was going on and at the height of our busyness, the telephone in its most demanding tone called me in from the garden one day. Arriving breathless I wiped a soily hand down my trousers and snatched it up. Then, as gently as I could, I announced myself.

'It's Mary,' said an equally level voice. 'I'm ringing, firstly, to let you know that Frances and I have arrived home and . . .' She hesitated, drawing in a deep breath. 'And secondly, to ask you if you've written that timetable yet.'

'Timetable?' I queried, guessing what was coming and playing for time.

'You know, that timetable of jobs, the one I suggested you make out for me.' She paused, this time for longer, and I unthinkingly let her wait for a moment whilst I collected together a whole medley of thoughts and feelings. 'To put it bluntly . . .' Her voice rose now, reverberating in my ear and then in a great spurt, words tumbled out: 'Can I come back . . . Please?'

Slowly, very slowly a warm glow pervaded me. 'When?' I asked.

'Next week?'

'*Next week*! But can you afford to?' This part of the request was unexpected and I found myself instantly taking stock of my reaction and even more surprisingly, found it to be one of supreme joy.

'May I, please? . . . Please?'

For the third time within ten minutes, Skerry is sitting stubbornly on the letter I'm trying to write. At the same moment, Mooskit has leaped on to the ledge of the dresser where I know for sure that he's threatening to pat something off with his paw. 'That is,' he says, 'if you don't, very soon, rise from your work and produce some food.' Flugga is clambering over my lap and butting my chin with his head, which is his way of saying the same thing; in short all three are being thoroughly objectionable. Meanwhile dear Tildy, once Mary's little dog, wise and knowing, her chin tucked comfortably between her paws, is darting me the odd glance, flashing the whites of her eyes and leaving all other guile to the cats.

'You're a horrible bullying lot,' I keep telling them. 'How on earth d'you think I'm going to write all these letters when I've to put up with such disgusting behaviour?' I don't think they're taking it in, of course . . . 'Look, pussies, couldn't you allow me just five minutes more?' No, it seems doubtful that they will, for apart from the muted ticking of the clock, a sullen, somewhat urgent silence has now permeated the room. I'm not going to be pressurised by it though, and determinedly pick up my pen, hoping at least to finish one more letter. Good, I've at last started . . . Whoops! Or have I? 'Skerry . . . do stop it! Skerry!' Oh, it's not good, I'm having to push one of his panther-paws off the pad continually. These contriving beasties have thoroughly outwitted me and I, having twisted around to glance at the timepiece, see anyway that I'm thoroughly outmanoeuvred. 'Oh, all right. Come on, it's almost time. You win, let's get it over with.'

No sooner am I on my feet than Flugga and Skerry instantly disappear, having canon-balled off in the direction of food. Mooskit pounces off the dresser and Tildy, who has clambered off her bean bag as fast as her short, shaggy legs will allow her, annoyingly brakes, half tripping me up. She now stretches luxuriously as I step over her, though she will waste no time in twinkling after us to the kitchen when she's had her yawn. The kitchen, which is tiny, hardly provides room for such a clan so, doling out four dishes of pet food as quickly as I can, I've placed each in its appropriate place so as to give myself room. The felines dine a pace or two away on the bottom of the stairs and Tildy, here on the kitchen floor. What a determined lot they are, I think to myself as I wash up dishes and dispose of two empty tins. Yet I know that I wouldn't be without any of them.

All four, amply satisfied now, are showing it in their own having-a-good-wash-licking-of-paws animal way, and will be content for hours. What lovely companionship they each individually give and in turn, in their response to human love, accept from us. Also, unlike humans, they seem to ask only for what they really need.

Long ago, a wise old friend maintained that the animal kingdom hadn't fallen nearly so far as we humans and I've a feeling he might have been right. I certainly believe that these 'lesser, lower, unintelligent creatures' as they are so often termed, can teach us a lot about the simple acceptance of our state.

I've just remembered that I promised to prepare this evening's supper and that Mary, now Sister Mary Clare, will be back any moment from visiting an elderly island friend. Having peered into the cupboard and found nothing obvious to eat that will make a simple meal, I must poke around somewhere else for something that won't cause me too much vexation of spirit for, as I've mentioned, I'm no cook.

Mooskit is sitting at the outside door and I'm trying not to let him see I've noticed, for I know quite well that he's willing me to open it for him and 'at once', giving me the 'poor little pleading pussy' treatment. For some reason he has a great aversion to cat-flaps, so . . . Ah well, I'd better pull out this tin of baked beans, which is the best I can do, and stretch over and open the door for him. If I don't make the effort, he will grudgingly use the flap. He is wise enough to know however that Sister Mary Clare and I have an extremely English attitude to our pets and understand his policy well, which is always to ask first. He squeaks as I push the door shut after him, for in a touching and slightly amusing way (we try not to laugh), he usually says 'Thank you'.

How lovely it is that, unlike us humans, our pets are uncomplicated. Also, although some folk say that they have no souls I'm of the opinion, and hopefully I'm not wrong, that any creature that is capable of loving does have something akin to one. Love, the kernel of life, is life's meaning, life's force, and is reflected in all things. Especially it is reflected in the meek and simple, in the little ones who accept life for what it is, glorying in it, in every breath, in simply being, in every blade of grass, in the warmth of the sun, in the song of a lark, in love and all that love is, and in Him who is Supreme Love . . .

The garden gate has just clicked, which probably means that Sister Mary Clare is home. Yes, here she is . . . Moving the saucepan on to the stove I light the gas.

'Hello, had a nice time, Sister?'

'Hello, yes, lovely thank you. Look, Leza's given us some of her *rhubarb and ginger jam . . . Oh, I see supper's about ready. Excuse me, I won't be a tick.'*

It's now five or six ticks later and we're sitting at the table. Grace said, we start our meal, as ever realising afresh how blessed we are. Blessed that God has called us both and the rest of our SOLI family to this wonderful simplicity, of living in Him.

> Love goes into God's presence unannounced,
>   while at the gate
> Reason and Knowledge must remain,
>   and for an audience wait.[1]

S for SNOWY OWL
Fetlar is well known for its Snowy Owl

3 A Flutter of Wings

'Yes of course you can, Mary, I'd love to have you. Bless you, you're welcome,' I told her over the telephone, coming to terms with my shock. 'That is, if you don't mind using Rosemary's little caravan which actually is in the process of being painted. The big one which you shared with Frances will be occupied next week.'

So it was that, exactly a week later, I met Mary again at the terminal along with my other guest. It was thrilling to see her and once she had settled into the timetable that I had concocted she was a tremendous help, especially with the cooking, which was the job that I most happily delegated.

The weather was glorious and we had another lovely week, this time working in the garden, entertaining guests and catching up on many of the jobs that I was behind with. Mary, full of joy, told me at some later date that one of the highlights of this second visit was that my very dear island friends Mimie and Kenny and Anne their daughter, who had only seen her fleetingly the week before, teasingly welcomed her back by saying, 'Long time no see!' 'It was then,' she told me, 'that strange as it may seem, I knew I belonged.'

There was a highlight for me too during this special week, and it happened one afternoon whilst I was in the neuk painting a baptismal candle. Needing to finish the candle and post it in time for a christening in Devon the following week, I was working under pressure. Suddenly I heard footsteps on the stairs, there was a tap on the door, and in came Mary with a mug of tea.

'What a marvellous surprise, that's just what I need. Thank you, Mary, you must be a thought reader.'

Putting the tea on the table she knelt down at my side and looked more closely at the candle. 'Mmm, it's lovely . . .'

'Won't you have a mug of tea too?' I asked. 'If so bring it up here.'

'Yes, thank you I will, though first, there's something I'd like to ask you and I hope you won't think me interfering.'

'Whatever is it? I'm intrigued.'

'Well it seems to me that you're looking worn out. Couldn't you have a day off whilst I'm here helping?'

'That's a lovely thought and I feel deeply touched by it. Though it isn't as easy, Mary, as it might seem. You see, there's several things like this candle for instance, that I can't put off doing. As well as four letters that simply must go out with the next post, not to mention urgent jobs in the garden. The problem is that Rosemary's away and I, being one very limited person at the centre of a life which is becoming increasingly busy, simply have to keep on.'

'But you mustn't. You're not that indispensable surely, not just for one day? You must stop, Sister, and take a break for every reason, for the sake of the work itself to start with.' Laying a hand on my free one, she looked pleadingly at me. 'Please Sister, say yes . . . Please . . .'

I was so moved by her concern that I knocked a tin of black paint all over my rug!

Towards the end of our lovely week, during which I did take a break, three rather special things happened. The first was a trip to Yell to attend a service in the most northerly parish church in the Anglican Communion which comes within Father Lewis' auspices as he is the only Episcopalian priest in Shetland. The church is a ferry ride and about twenty miles' drive south-west of Fetlar. I have already described our old banger of a car which, banger or no, was a necessary mode of transport to us. What I have not yet mentioned is that it could only do, at the very maximum, seventeen miles per run. It functioned perfectly until it had done its quota. At that point it would simply stutter to a halt, leaving its passengers to sit for anything between fifteen minutes and two hours. Once the allotted period of time had elapsed there was no problem – it roared abruptly into motion and off it went. So it was not surprising that under these circumstances, in an isolated spot amongst the peaty hills of Yell, we juddered to a stop. 'Don't worry,' I said to Mary and my other guest, 'this is usual.'

An hour later Mary laid aside the piece of embroidery that she was working on and peered over her specs. 'The only thing I know about motor car engines is how to clean the sparking plugs,' she proffered. 'Would you like me to have a go?'

'I'm sure it won't help or make the slightest difference . . . and I mean that of course very respectfully. On the other hand I'm sure it won't do any harm . . . Yes, do have a go.'

Smilingly, Mary squeezed out of the back seat whilst I scuffled around and found her a piece of rag. Taking it from me, she walked in a businesslike manner to the front of the car and after a few minutes poked a beaming face around the propped-up bonnet to call out. 'Try her now.' Putting down my book I condescendingly pulled out the starter, not a bit prepared for the immediate roar of the engine. 'Wow!' shrieked our newly-enlisted mechanic. 'It worked.'

'Jump in!' I yelled. 'Let's go.' The car moved off as though nothing had happened and within a few minutes we had arrived at our half-way stopping place where we had arranged to have lunch with two close friends of mine, Alma and Dennis, and their daughter Katie. Alma and Dennis, staunch members of the little church, St Colman's, to which we were going, had befriended me almost as soon as I had arrived in Shetland in 1984.

Our being late for the meal mattered not a jot to either of them who are always homely, welcoming and good-tempered. Consequently we had a jolly, if quick lunch together before setting off for the church which was another good car journey away. Our conveyance started without a whimper and we arrived for the service in good time. It was lovely to worship with our Episcopalian friends and afterwards to chat with them and to Father Lewis at the church door. After a while, seeing that Mary was having what appeared to be a serious talk with Lewis, I slipped off to wait in the car, leaving them to it. My other guest had stayed in church too so, happy to have a moment on my own, I closed my eyes. I was not to indulge long though, for, jolted out of my reverie by a sharp tap on the window, I saw Father Lewis. Winding down the window I grinned with surprise.

'What a nice person Mary is.' He spoke eagerly and then continued in a whisper, 'What do you think?'

'With regard to vocation?' I asked. He nodded, and looking around to see if she was within earshot I whispered back, 'I think it's escapism!'

We had yet another two breakdowns journeying home over Yell and had to call upon Dennis for help. Fortunately he was there right behind us in his own car; after a conference of war we arranged, along with Alma, that he would drop her off at their home and then return to us with a tow rope. This he quickly did and then very nobly towed us to the ferry where he suggested we abandon the car. 'A friend of mine will help me get it to a garage for you,' he promised. 'There's no point in taking it back to Fetlar.'

Thanking him profusely the three of us boarded the boat as foot passengers and sailed back to our isle. After docking I rang up a Fetlar friend who kindly said that she would drive at once to the ferry and pick us up.

Within half an hour Nana arrived and we piled thankfully into her car. However, to my consternation, I realised just before we turned the last corner for home, that I had left the key to The Ness in the car on Yell. Also, of course, that the next ferry over the six-mile stretch of sea would not be returning until the next day. I could have kicked myself, for to start with, where was I going to sleep? Mary was in the small caravan which was too small to share with another person, and our other friend was in the big caravan. Of course I knew that I could spend the night at Lower Ness, for although Rosemary was still away she would never mind me using her home. Oh dear, though, far more serious to me – what about the cats? Although, they had a cat-flap and so could get in and out, how was I to feed them? How also was I to feed my guests?

'I know, let's all have a cup of tea in the big caravan,' Mary suggested, 'before Nana goes.'

'Good idea, whilst I mull over what best to do,' I agreed. I love challenges and am absolutely convinced that nothing is impossible.

When no immediate answer presented itself I gulped down

the remains of my tea, excused myself from the burble of conversation and scooted back to The Ness. I twisted the knob sharply and battered the fiendish door with my shoulder, wanting to be absolutely certain that I had actually locked it. Yes, it was definitely locked. I peered in through the window of the porch/kitchen. There was no way of getting through any of the windows. Just a moment, though – shading my eyes I peered harder into the tiny room. Yes, there on the side was definitely my answer: the second key was sitting on a wooden ledge, about three feet high, to the right of the door and only a few feet from it.

'Mary!' I yelled in the direction of the caravan. 'Mary, could you come and help me, please?'

When she arrived, she found me fiddling around in the barn, groping amongst an old bundle of fencing materials for a long piece of wire. 'This'll do,' I shouted triumphantly, shaking it at her.

'Why? What . . .?'

'Just hold it at this end, whilst I twist the other into a loop,' I instructed her excitedly. 'After that, I'll explain what I want us to do.' The six-foot piece of wire was soon looped and the rest of it then bent into an L-shape so as to make the manoeuvre easier. That's good . . . now let me tell you. I've just spotted that the second key to the door is on a ledge in the kitchen, so if you'll go round and stand by the window, I'll lie on my tummy and wangle the wire through the cat-flap, while you shout out a few instructions.'

She dashed round the corner and directed operations marvellously. 'Left . . . Now right a bit, no, slightly back to the left . . . Now up . . . Up a bit more . . . Lovely, now across and down . . . Down! Good, you've got it, now sweep it on to the floor.'

Knocking the key off the ledge I scraped it along the floor until it was near enough to reach with an arm stretched at full length through the flap. Then grasping it in my hand I pulled it out, stood upright and jubilantly opened the door. After this I could only turn to a beaming Mary and throw my arms around her.

'Well,' she teased, 'we do work well together don't we?'

That evening, most unusually, Mary went missing. One hour, then two hours ticked away. Maybe she had gone off for a walk, I brooded, yet it was strange and unlike her not to have told me where she was going. One of the things which we have always asked of our visitors, is to give us a rough indication of the direction in which they're heading, if they are journeying far on their own. We think it is sensible to have at least an idea of the location folk might be in, in case they should get into difficulties. However, on this occasion I need not have worried, for on my way to Compline Mary hoved to.

'I'll join you in just two minutes,' she called out cheerfully, unaware of the anxiety she had caused.

'Good,' I replied and at the same time noticed an expression on her face that made me enquire after her departing form if she were all right.

'More than I've ever been,' she smiled, half turning towards me, then as an afterthought, 'I've been sitting in chapel thinking!'

The next day we worked together on Rosemary's caravan, finishing off the exterior painting. Unusually for Shetland, the day was hot with the midges biting hard. Having been told by someone that the best way of keeping them off was to stick a piece of mint behind one's ears, we picked bunches of it from the garden. Then we pushed bits into every accessible place, Mary into her hair, behind her specs, and I into my wimple and up my sleeves. We looked ridiculous, I especially with sprigs sticking out of my headband. Despite being hot and grossly irritated by the insects we were happy, and Mary again spoke in general terms of her future. She went on to ask what I felt the future held for me.

'Well, that very much depends on the first person whom God sends to join me . . .' I began. 'When I see who she is, then maybe I'll have a better glimpse of what the future holds. It's like this, you see . . .'

I told her of the three possible ways in which I saw the years ahead developing. I could stay as a solitary with a group of Caim members associated loosely with me. Or, if like-minded

29

souls asked to join me, requesting a deeper and specific commitment, we could form a community of solitaries. Or thirdly, if a different type of aspirant presented herself, or should I say, if God sent her to me, this could mean that a mixed life of prayer and action should be embraced. Skirting around the second two options I concentrated at this point on the first – the associate group to which close friends, like Alma and Dennis, belonged. 'It's called the Caim, and as you probably know, *Caim* is a Celtic word meaning encompassment or "the circle around". In our case it's a circle of friends who support us by their prayers, living their own lives, in their own homes in and around Great Britain.' Mary looked interested. No, she looked more than interested, enough so to make me blurt out quite without meaning to, 'You're not interested in joining the Caim are you?'

'No, certainly not,' she returned. 'That's not what I want, what I want is something more . . .' She hesitated. 'I want to be that first person to join you as a Sister.'

Inwardly I reeled, though after a moment's hesitation I threw down my paintbrush, bounded to her side and hugged my first, extremely minty-smelling, aspirant. A moment later I stood back. 'Are you really sure?'

'Yes, I am.'

'And if I say yes, would you be prepared to speak about this with both the Bishop of Aberdeen and Orkney who is my guardian and with Father Lewis, who as you know is my spiritual director?'

'Yes I would,' she said.

'More than that, would you also be prepared to wait for one year from now, before actually joining me? It's a tough life up here and we need, on both sides, to be as sure as we can that there's a real call.'

'I'm sure now.' She was emphatic, 'I knew last night, in chapel.'

Towards the end of this piquant week, the third incident happened, and it was all bound up with the East Kirk bell that had been given me by the island people. The gift had arrived approximately a year after the kirk had been converted into the island's community hall. The bell, a beautiful one, greatly loved by many of the islanders and with a lovely tone, had hung in the bell tower of the old building since it had been erected. Faithfully it had tolled out its sonorous voice, Sunday after Sunday, over the croftlands of the isle. That is, until the congregations of the east and west kirks were, I understand somewhat painfully, amalgamated and the building became obsolete as a church. So during its latter years the tongue of the large bell had hung silent. I did not witness the taking down of it, which included the demolishing of the tower, though I heard that ropes were tied around the masonry, hooked on to a JCB, and with a mighty roar the whole edifice including the bell was detached from the building. After this, it lay for months on a grassy verge by the side of the road, looking pathetically abandoned. Needless to say a fair amount of damage was done, though not as much as might have been expected. The rope wheel was bent double and is now virtually useless, though one day we hope to have it restored. However, the bell itself was lying at this juncture of my story in the byre/chapel waiting for me to find someone (I had Bob the postman in mind) to hang it in an appropriate place. Despite its smashed wheel I thought that in some way we could manage to ring and use it.

'When do you think you'll get the bell up?' Mary asked me one morning.

'Well, I'm really waiting for Bob to come and give me some advice,' I told her, 'and I've a feeling that the actual erection of the bell is, well, quite a long way off.'

'Why don't you put it up yourself then? I mean temporarily. I'd give you a hand . . . Oh do let me, I'm sure you could do it and I could be quite handy at handing nails.'

Busy though I was, how could I refuse such an inventive challenge? 'All right, and since there's no time like the present, let's get started. There's just about an hour before the midday Office.'

Fired by enthusiasm we found a few wooden fencing stakes, some planks of wood, a hammer and a box of nails. Then, with Mary handing me these various items at the appropriate moments, a strong frame high enough to take the bell was soon erected and roofed over. We built it bell-tower style in a small triangular piece of garden at the back of the byre/chapel.

During the afternoon, whilst totally engrossed in this fascinating project, we were suddenly aware that we were not alone. For, striding across the vegetable garden on the other side of the triangle was the friend who had rebuffed me down at the ferry. To my astonishment she announced that she had come to tell me a few home truths. And the first? That I was a fraud! Mary, horrified and embarrassed, slipped silently into the byre/chapel, wondering as she did so whether she should have stayed to protect me. However, after my visitor had had her say and left, Mary appeared from the quiet shadows of her sanctuary.

'Look,' I murmured feeling somewhat shaken, 'let's go into the house and I'll make us a strong cup of tea.'

'No, come to Rosemary's little caravan instead and I'll make the tea,' she insisted.

A moment or two later we had our first heart-to-heart conversation when I was able to explain that our visitor, through some strange misconception, did not think me an authentic religious.

'But I don't understand the reasoning of it all,' said Mary, bewildered.

'I think I do,' I said. 'You see, when things begin to go well, such as your asking to join me yesterday and my suddenly knowing that it could be the right thing . . . Well, it's rather as though a spanner has to be thrown into the works. Though that in itself could of course be a sign that one is actually on the right track.'

'Yes,' she agreed, 'and it's almost as though that started to happen from the moment that I landed on Fetlar. I didn't like to tell you before, but that same lady chatted to me on the ferry when we first arrived. I asked her if she was on her way to stay with you as we were and she said no she most certainly was not. Then she told us that you weren't a real Sister . . . I was a bit taken aback I can tell you, and that's why I had a few serious words with Father Lewis on Sunday. There were one or two very straight questions that I needed to ask him, and one was "If somebody wanted to join Sister Agnes would you discourage them?"'

'So what did he answer?'

'He looked at me, absolutely straight in the eye, and stated simply and firmly "No!"'

Smiling, I thought what a good champion of my cause Father Lewis was and how blessed I was to have such a director as he.

'Look,' I said, 'if you would like to speak about this to anyone else in authority, that is, before you commit yourself further, you're at perfect liberty to do so . . . You do know that, don't you? I'd absolutely understand.'

Her response was immediate. 'No, no, I'm more decided than ever and don't need to question a soul.'

The next day I waved a sad farewell to Mary, feeling what a pity it was that she and Rosemary still had not met. The really aggravating thing this time, though, was that their ships were to pass in the middle of the night somewhere between Lerwick and Aberdeen.

Rosemary was beaming as brightly as the August morning when I collected her. 'I say,' she said, as I helped her with her suitcases off the ferry. 'D'you know, one of the very nicest things about going away for a holiday is the coming back home again . . . Has anything exciting happened whilst I've been away?'

'One or two things. I'll catch you up on some of them as we drive along. And yes, I do agree about coming home. In fact, I don't need to tell you this, I can hardly bear to leave the island even to go shopping.'

Soon after our arrival home, when Rosemary had dug herself back into Lower Ness and had been reunited with Kelpie, I took her out to the byre/chapel garden to show her the newly-erected bell.

'How on earth did you manage to lift that heavy bell on to the frame? It must have taken at least a couple of men. Did you say that Mary helped you?'

'Rosemary, you'll be very shocked and perhaps a little angry . . . but I did it myself.'

'You blighter, I might have known . . . absolutely typical. How?'

'Well, I knew that if I'd have asked someone to help me they would have insisted that the bell was too heavy to lift. So I arranged for Mary and our guest to go off to tea with Leza, knowing that Leza's sort of hospitality would keep them away for as long as I needed.'

'Mmm, clever. Though what then?'

'The first thing I had to do was to rig up a ramp, which I did just here, right underneath the frame. That wasn't too difficult because I had an old box and a large piece of board that were exactly the right size. It was the next bit that proved tiresome, for I had to roll the bell over and over through the byre/chapel, out through the door and then across the garden to the bottom of the ramp. Since it was a fair weight this part of the operation made me infuriatingly slow. However, after I'd achieved those two things I simply tied a long piece of strong rope around the supporting bar, leaving a loop of it dangling at the right sort of height to catch the shoulder of the bell. Then I heaved the bell up the ramp until I was able to flick the loop into place. All that I needed to do then, of course, was to finish tying the rope around the shoulders and when it was really secure, push away the ramp.'

'You're *very* naughty, though I do think it's a lovely piece of work,' was Rosemary's honest opinion.

'Thank you, Rosemary. For that, I'll let you ring the Angelus on it at twelve o'clock.'

As she stood, continuing to admire, we noticed a car wending its way down our road to The Ness. As it passed the end of the garden we gazed at each other thoughtfully, for we saw that it was full of waving people.

'I'll slip indoors and put the kettle on if you'd kindly greet them,' I murmured.

The visitors from the Shetland Mainland were taking some English relatives on a grand tour around Shetland. 'We thought it'd be nice to come over to Fetlar, see a wee bit of the island and pay you a quick call,' said one of the ladies of the party as she delved into a basket. 'We've brought you this . . .' She handed over a large home-made fruit cake.

'How super of you,' I exclaimed, taking it from her. Thank you . . . Let's have it with our cup of tea, shall we? And let's have both out here in the garden, in this wonderful sunshine.'

As I poured out the last cup of tea I noticed, from the corner of my eye, the figure of a woman passing the edge of The Ness boundary, and appearing to be heading in the direction of the beach. She did not look our way, though I saw immediately that it was the friend who had rebuked me two days before. Making a quick and rather daring decision, knowing that if the risk did not come off I could be ridiculed in front of all our visitors, I stood up, waving the teapot. 'Come and join us for a cup of tea,' I yelled. She turned, hesitated, and then to my disappointment disappeared from view. However it was only to reappear a moment or two later and, with great grace, join us.

The only vacant seat was beside me on the garden bench and after I had introduced her to the other visitors we sat there, sipping tea and chatting amicably enough. That was, until our guests rose from their seats saying that they must depart. It was at this point, during the noise of the departure, that my friend turned and whispered urgently to me.

'You suggested, when we were speaking the other day in the garden, that if I wanted to say something of a serious nature then we'd better go into the house and have a proper talk, privately. I'd like to do this, so if we could make some kind of an appointment I'd be grateful.'

I suggested that she came later that same afternoon, which she did, and at our interview a great misunderstanding with regard to my authenticity was cleared up. In fact we ended our session by saying the prayer of St Francis of Assisi together.

The next day was a Fetlar post day, always a joy as we only have three posts a week, and in it was a postcard from Mary, postmarked Aberdeen. She had written it before turning in, on her fourteen-hour voyage between Lerwick and the Scottish Mainland.

11th August 1988

Thank you . . . and a definite *Yes* – an unequivocal commitment for my part.
Yours in Christ,
Mary.

P.S. I'm singing too!!

I'm sitting in the but room, mending, feeling the warmth of the sun across my shoulders and even in this piece of fabric over which I'm bent. Every so often I can't help but glance around at my surroundings. For from the first moment I ever set foot in them I thought of this room as an especially dear place. The low beams give it character and the large fireplace which, unfortunately, has had to have its chimney blocked up, has now an electric fire set into it which gives a feeling of cosiness. Even its walls seem to exude a warmth and peace which makes me wonder if perhaps the souls who've lived here over the centuries have known something of real joy. Have women folk knelt here before the hearth speaking to God familiarly, as the generations of the Isles were wont to do, speaking to him as a friend as they smoored the peats? Did they ask blessings on their home and their flocks, their cattle and their dear ones? Did these gentle northerners not only carry the thought of their Creator in their hearts but also know him intimately in their midst, in Jesus his Son and in Mary the mother of Jesus and in all the saints of these shores? And I wonder, did they say such prayers as this:

> The peace of God, the peace of men,
> The peace of Columba kindly,
> The peace of Mary mild, the loving,
> The peace of Christ, King of tenderness,
>   The peace of Christ, King of tenderness,
>
> Be upon each window, upon each door,
> Upon each hole that lets in light,
> Upon the four corners of my house,
> Upon the four corners of my bed,
>   Upon the four corners of my bed;
>
> Upon each thing my eye takes in,
> Upon each thing my mouth takes in,
> Upon my body that is of earth
> And upon my soul that came from on high,
>   Upon my body that is of earth
>   And upon my soul that came from on high.[1]

Skerry has joined me now and has just leaped on to the couch on the right-hand side of the fireplace. The couch, or chaise longue as we sometimes call it, is old and has sat in its present position for as long as the most elderly of my local friends can remember. It's not comfortable, yet we would not move it, or stop using, it for worlds. Sister Mary Clare has made a beautiful pastel-coloured cover, which we've spread over its dark leather seat and which now merges its bulk into the walls of the room and throws into relief its woodwork.

Across from the couch is the window, which looks out into a small garden surrounded by a dry stone dyke. Through its panes I watch branches of red fuchsias sway in the breeze, waving their arms every so often above the wall, so contrasting their brilliance against a background of blue sea. Yes, the window frames the scene beautifully with its sill of geraniums and Busy Lizzies now a riot of colour and in the midst of these, contrasting again, is the dark green, glossy *foliage of a camellia without bud. Yet in a month or so, at Christmas time, when the days are dark, the birds flown, the lark's song only a memory and the garden barren, for the icy winds will have bleached this northern clime of even its green grass, then, like Isaiah's rose in the desert, our winter-flowering camellia will bloom and in it we'll be glad.*

> *The wilderness and the solitary place shall be glad for them; and the desert shall rejoice and blossom as a rose. It shall blossom abundantly, and rejoice even with joy and singing.*[2]

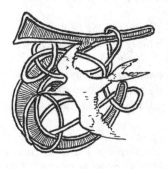

T for TERN

4 Dark Winged Sky

'I've a right pile for you today,' smiled Bob the postman, handing me a bulge of letters held together with two rubber bands.

'Oh Bob, I haven't answered the last lot yet. I do think you might have held a few back till I have.'

I sat down in the sunshine on the bench under the but room window and sliced open a dozen envelopes. There was one with Mary's handwriting spread thickly across it and I opened that first. 'Ah, good,' I muttered to myself when I found that she was asking if she might still come up for the October half term break. 'And,' she added: 'You'll be interested to know that I'm not wanting any guarantees about getting back this time!'

One of the other letters that day was from an Australian woman named Rosemary, who later we were to call Rose so as to differentiate her from our Rosemary of Lower Ness. Rose, a born nurse, had been writing to me for a couple of years, having read an article describing my life in Shetland. Apparently, one night whilst on duty in the hospice where she worked, she tried to keep herself awake by flicking through a pile of magazines. From one of them, this particular feature leaped from the pages and stimulated her imagination. So much did it inflame her that the next day she wrote to me, not with the idea of becoming anything as silly as a Sister but just simply because she was interested in Fetlar – interested in it geographically and in my vision of forming a new community on the island.

Later, I was to discover that not only was Rose deeply dedicated to her nursing, but she was also a deeply committed Christian and, interestingly, her forebears, she told me, were of Scottish origin. Looking again at the letter which contained the final arrangements regarding her now imminent visit, I memorised her times. Then, folding the pages, I smiled to myself, for despite the gentle soul that she sounded, she stated in the last paragraph in no uncertain manner that she wanted me to know that she definitely did *not* have a vocation to the religious life.

Rose was due to arrive on Fetlar the following week and, very conveniently as it turned out, so was an old college friend of Rosemary's. Since they were to be travelling on the same ship we suggested that they look out for each other. This they did, so that when the ship anchored on the Shetland Mainland they had company on the long coach and inter-island ferry journeys up to the north.

The morning of their arrival dawned and as planned Rosemary and I drove to the Fetlar ferry to meet them. No sooner had we arrived than the boat slid in and as it docked we craned our necks to see Rose and Noreen amongst the passengers waiting to come off. Surprisingly, there was no sign of either.

'Oh dear, they must have missed the coach from Lerwick,' cried Rosemary.

'Yes it rather looks as though they have,' I agreed. 'Maybe the St Clair was late arriving . . . though that would seem strange since the weather's so good. Ah well, they're certainly not here, so let's go home and make some telephone calls.'

We watched a couple of cars being waved on to the ferry, turned and seated ourselves in our own vehicle. 'Just a minute.' I pulled on the handbrake. 'They could have missed the overland bus but equally so, they could still be on the boat downstairs in the saloon.' We bounced out of the car again in time to see the ramp of the boat rising.

'Hi,' shouted Rosemary to the ferry man operating it. 'Hi, have you two passengers for Fetlar still on board?'

'Just a moment,' he called back good-temperedly and turned towards the steps that descended into the base of the boat. At exactly the same moment two heads bobbed into view, followed by two bodies each clutching a piece of luggage and a book. The ferry man sighed, pressed a button and instantly the ramp creaked slowly down and locked itself back into position. Waving, we hastened forward and took their bags.

'You haven't been sitting downstairs *reading*?' They nodded.

'Well I'm appalled,' spluttered Rosemary. 'On your first visit to Fetlar too. Were you *really* down there, in the bowels of the boat? Didn't you want to enjoy the scenery and your first glimpse of the island?' Poor Rose and Noreen, they had been so engrossed in their books that neither of them had even realised that the boat had arrived.

We lifted Noreen's baggage into the back of the car and slammed down the hatchback. Rose, who was travelling impressively light, tucked hers neatly in beside her on the back seat and the rest of us jumped in.

We both instantly liked Rose. 'Now, she's the kind of person who would make a lovely Sister,' Rosemary whispered to me later as we washed up the lunch things.

'Shush, don't say that too loudly,' I hissed. 'It's the very last thing she wants.'

Rose was with us for a week and as the days progressed I could see her becoming more and more preoccupied. Apparently at a crossroads in her life with regard to her nursing career, she wanted time and space to think and possibly to do some decision-making.

In such time as I could find, I showed Rose something of the island; in fact, on one of her days we had a crazy picnic which ended in a deluge of rain and found ourselves thoroughly enjoying it although, needless to say, it had not been planned that way. More and more she grew to love Fetlar and to relate to the simplicity of our life here. Excitedly, I talked to her about Mary's coming and of all our hopes and plans for the future, and I think something of the joy of it seeped into her being.

Again, as with Mary and Frances, time accelerated towards the day of her departure and as it did so, she became increasingly pensive. Nothing would persuade me to encourage or discourage anyone about joining SOLI, for that, I feel, is entirely the Lord's prerogative. However, it came as no surprise to be handed an envelope the day before she left, containing one of the loveliest letters that I have ever been privileged to receive. In it she explained how she was finding it easier to write rather than to say what she felt she must, especially since the whole thing was totally incomprehensible to her mind and the last thing she had planned. It seemed that the Lord was in some way suggesting that she think seriously about attaching herself to us in some way.

I had told Mary that she must wait a year in order to be sure, and when I spoke to Rose I said the same thing, that is, that a time of preparation was essential. Readily she agreed and I began to sense that my little community in embryo was coming together with some splendid women.

Rose departed feeling somewhat stunned and I, on cloud nine, began to work out in a vague sort of way how I was going to accommodate two extra people in The Ness the following year.

Upon this subject, my thoughts returned again and again to Brough Lodge, a great empty pile of a building situated in one of the most beautiful spots on Fetlar and which, unless restored soon, would be beyond all hope of renovation.

'I'll give you that it's a very romantic idea,' whispered a sensible little voice in my head, 'though please don't overlook the fact that it would cost thousands of pounds to repair and after you've done that, what would you have? Nothing more than a pseudo-baronial hall. Anyhow, the new inheritor of the property probably won't dream of selling. And what, may I ask, would you buy it with if she did – the three hundred pounds you've saved in the bank? That, of course, would go a long way, though would not I think stretch to having the castellated roof restored, or the lookout tower made into a hermitage for retreat, or the chapel which, as you know, is at the moment used as a hay barn, rebuilt – and what about the courtyard? Yes, now, the courtyard . . . Mmm . . . yes . . . I *say* d'you know, I think, you might be right . . . Yes, you could be, and it could just work . . . Let's look at the whole thing from your point of view then. The courtyard could be converted into a super cloister, in fact the whole place has simply everything you might need and more. It's large enough for a small group of Sisters and a few guests, though isn't too large or pretentious as mansions go . . .'

'Stop it!' I yelled at my inner voice. 'Don't encourage me, because for a start it's quite the wrong image. I want ordinary folk to be able to relate to the community. I want the community to be simple, not strung around with enormous debts of a white elephant house, and as you've just intimated, I've hardly enough to live on without buying such things.'

'Yes, yes I understand all of *that* perfectly,' my voice persisted, 'though I was under the impression that it is *you* who always maintains that if a door opens, however slightly, then one should look behind it.'

'Oh, all right, you win, but I warn you, I'm not going to do more than have the tiniest peep.'

My 'peep' consisted in writing a note to the new owner of the property, a lady who with her husband lives and works in Scotland. 'I'm probably mad,' I scratched away, 'but Brough has all that we would seem to need . . .' I then went on to tell her my position and asked her if she would ever consider selling the house and gardens. How pleased I was when a gentle answer came back a week or so later, stating that she absolutely understood and sympathised with my predicament though she felt, sadly, that the aunt from whom she had inherited the property would not have liked her to sell it. In any case, until such time as it was out of the hands of the lawyers she could make no plans at all for it. My reaction to all this was not of disappointment but of instant relief. No, there was nothing, or so it seemed, behind the doors of Brough.

The summer came rapidly to an end and very soon autumn was upon us with Mary back for her week's half-term break. We walked and talked much about the future. She had already burned her boats with regard to the Canadian post by asking to have her name removed from the list. So consequently, her October week with me was a very challenging one. Strangely, it was very similar, in its painfulness and heart searching, to my own first ten days on Fetlar, when I too had had to come to terms with my decision to come and live here. In my case, I had had to accept wholly what I believed was a call from God and then, torn apart, return to Devon to ask permission from my Order to come back to this northerly, remote little outpost. All of that had taken great courage – and now it was Mary's turn.

In my own wrestlings I had gone to Halliara-kirk, an ancient church site situated on top of the hill behind The Ness. Virtually nothing is known about this strange, holy place where all that remains is a grassy knoll, a few scattered rocks, the crumbling walls of a tiny building, probably nothing to do with its religious past, a tremendous view over the island and an incredibly strong feel of the past. It is what I call my 'thinking place' and is where I head if I have any important decisions to make. It was alone there, on that first visit to Fetlar in 1983, that I had confirmed my Yes, to God. So one afternoon during Mary's tense week I was not a bit surprised when she suggested that we take a walk up the hill to that special place.

I said nothing of my feelings for it as we climbed up the hill, in fact we were both heavily silent. Glancing around and occasionally back at The Ness, now minute in the distance, we were not unaware of dark clouds speeding above us. Halliara-kirk was dressed in a strangely funereal garb and seemed as bleak that day as I have ever known it. Only Mary could tell fully what agonies of indecision she went through when we arrived. Indeed, I also had experienced there and was now in part sharing with her a sharp, cutting, cleansing experience. Reaching the top we stood and in a strange way waited for we hardly knew what. Then, unable to bear the tension any longer, I reached out hesitantly to touch her hand as a gesture of support, unintentionally opening the floodgates in her and she wept. Feeling utterly dejected myself I stood aside, refusing to believe that there was any doubt as to her call, though afterwards, and despite my efforts to maintain my belief, I remember walking home feeling the pain of a possible bereavement.

The week swiftly ended in a sombre way until on the last evening, as we stood in the porch/kitchen waiting for the kettle to boil, Mary, in great elation, suddenly embraced me.

'There's something that I've been bursting to tell you all day. I haven't, because I was afraid that I was incapable of getting the importance and the wonder of it over to you in words.' She paused, flushed and excited, and I waited silently until she was ready to continue. 'You see, this morning whilst I was having a tub – and it's hard to believe that it happened there –

well, my vocation became lucidly clear.' She laughed and went on, 'It was such a funny place to have a revelation, yet it was *so* special that I simply can't describe it. I'll never forget it, Sister, ever, and what I'm sure about it is, that it wouldn't have been nearly so special if I hadn't had all those doubts.'

'Mary, I'm so thrilled for you and for SOLI, and for myself,' I cried. 'That's wonderful.'

She hugged me again and involuntarily, not meaning to, I stiffened. Noticing it immediately she unlocked me from her grasp, stretched me away to her arms' length and looked at me straight. After a moment's pause she spoke quietly and distinctly. 'I haven't studied psychology for nothing and I'd like you to know that, in spite of your twenty-plus years in a convent, for me, touch is very important.' For once I was speechless and felt more vulnerable than I ever had. 'There's something else that I want you to know,' she went on. 'I want to share with you what my Bible reading was today, which I read in the early hours of this morning. It was about Ruth and Naomi . . . about real trust and real friendship from Ruth 1:14 and 16. Would you read it too, and share my joy?' Something inside me snapped, long over-due and long needed. Nodding, I promised that I would, and we said goodnight.

The next day at the crack of dawn we said the early morning Office of Prime in the oratory. Afterwards, on a sudden impulse, I rose from my knees and standing by Mary placed my hands on her head.

> 'May the Lord bless you and keep you, Mary.
> May he make his face to shine upon you
> And be gracious unto you until we meet again,
> May the Lord bless you, dear Mary.'

She looked up, her eyes shining. 'Thank you . . . so much, Sister,' she whispered.

After breakfast, very sadly, I drove her to the ferry, and on coming home found a little note with a beautifully embroidered bookmark enclosed from her. The bookmark had been the one she had been working at on the day that our car had broken down on Yell. Later, I placed it into my Bible to mark the Ruth and Naomi chapter. A bond had been formed.

Tucked warmly into my bed in a corner of the neuk, I'm enjoying the swinging light that is spasmodically illuminating the room. The night's a furious one, and a fishing boat seeking shelter is anchored out in the Wick. Its mast, visible above the hillock that divides The Ness from the inlet, has a light attached at its highest point, and as the small vessel lifts on the billows it sends gleams of movement and companionship into the night.

The Ness, set on an isolated point, is dark in the winter, that is except during the nights of the full moon. Then, in her too, I find comforting companionship. Especially I found this to be so, when I lived here alone. Perhaps she was, as the Celts would have described her, 'a friend of great love'.[1]

Yet, however other souls have thought of her, for me the moon is a great symbol of our God who is all Love and all Light, the God of whom St Paul says: 'For God, who commanded the light to shine out of darkness, hath shined in our hearts, to give the light of the know-ledge of the glory of God in the face of Jesus Christ.'[2]

In the face of Jesus shines a type of moon, a type of sun, and He, the Light of the World, the Son of God, calls us in turn to be truly the sons and daughters of Light, to shine in the dark. We're very aware of the darkness of sin, sometimes our own sin, as it drifts ceaselessly across the world. Yet it's a darkness, which we know is like the cloud covering the moon. However much cloud, the moon is still there and though its light be hidden it is not extinguished.

My eyelids fall heavy now and soon, hardly before I know it, the sunlight has crept into the room.

> *The eye of the great God,*
> *The eye of the God of glory,*
> *The eye of the King of hosts,*
> *The eye of the King of the living,*
> *Pouring upon us*
> *At each season,*
> *Pouring upon us*
> *Gently and generously.*
>
> *Glory to thee,*
> *Thou glorious sun.*
>
> *Glory to thee, thou sun,*
> *Face of the God of life.*[3]

With a wiggle I stretch my limbs as gently as I can between the weight of two, or is it three, sleeping cats. There is a twitter of birdsong and I give thanks.

5 Return to the Nest

Amazingly, Mary managed to raise enough money to return to Shetland again for her next school holiday. By this time it was almost Christmas, and since the Bishop of Aberdeen and Orkney was coming up to the Northern Isles to conduct an ordination we arranged a meeting between him and Mary in Lerwick soon after her term ended.

An ordination is a rare thing up here in Shetland, and this one, to the diaconate, was of a friend of mine, Liz, who not only worked as a children's dentist in Lerwick but also assisted Father Lewis in his work at St Magnus. Father Lewis had arranged that Liz should have a retreat before her great day and had kindly invited me to join the little group of five. A large country house, beautifully situated on the Shetland Mainland, and usually used for conferences, was duly booked and the Provost of Aberdeen Cathedral flew up to take the retreat for us. It was a treasured experience, and most especially I enjoyed the opportunity of walking in the hills around the house and really having time to think both about the future and about my own vocation.

The evening before the ordination our retreat ended and we all drove into Lerwick. There, Liz dropped me off at the home of Catherine, a church member, where I was to be given lodgings for two nights. Actually, by this time I was just longing to be home and feeling tremendously excited that Mary would be accompanying me. Mary was to arrive on the St Clair the next morning and had also been invited by Liz to the ordination service and reception. So, as arranged, early the next morning she was collected by another church friend off the ship and brought along to join me in my abode. She arrived beaming with pleasure and there, perkily trotting after her, was Matilda, her dog. Matilda, or Tildy for short, is a small Australian terrier of whom Mary is very fond. So fond, in fact, that wanting to be sure that she would fit into our Fetlar family she had brought her up to meet us all. Instantly I was captivated, and had a feeling that even the cats might welcome this gentle, lovable creature – at least I hoped that they would after their initial shock.

After a lovely service and reception we returned to our lodgings, for Catherine, very kindly, had also offered Mary a bed for the night. Mary was tired after her travelling, though we managed to catch up on much news.

Morning dawned full of thoughts of Fetlar, though first, before our departure, we had to see the bishop. Bishop Frederick had become a good friend and had been a marvellous spiritual support to me over the few years that I had known him. Indeed, had it not been for the blessing that he had bestowed on me when I first asked to live within his diocese, many miracles on Fetlar would not have happened – or not in the way that they have. He joined us mid-morning at Catherine's where we had a cup of coffee together and then each spent some time privately with him. Mary, later as Sister Mary Clare, swore that I was given the first interview on this occasion to make sure that he asked her all the things that I wanted him to. She was not quite right, but I have never gone into it fully with her! Afterwards we were given a wonderful celebratory lunch by our hostess – celebrating the official acceptance by Bishop Frederick, Father Lewis and myself, of Mary, to the Aspirancy of SOLI.

Immediately after our meal, Father Lewis had arranged that we should be driven by the bishop as far as Yell, which is where I had left our car (the one that had been such a beastly pain!) and where the bishop was to take a pre-Christmas carol service at St Colman's. It would have been lovely to have gone to the service with him, but we would most certainly have missed the last ferry of the day had we done so.

As it was, having said an affectionate farewell to him and moved our baggage from one car to the other, we sped over Yell to arrive at the terminal with barely a minute to spare. By this time the evening had turned wintry and we were wondering how Tildy was going to cope with a rough crossing. Quickly we were waved on to the boat and carefully, with dipped headlights, I manoeuvred the car up and over the ramp. This was always a nerve-racking experience in this vehicle, for it was infuriatingly low-slung and it was almost impossible not to catch the exhaust pipe on the metal ridge where the ramp was hinged to the ferry. A few other Fetlar cars were already in position, so sliding in behind them we settled ourselves for the dark half-hour journey. As the boat shuddered out into the ocean Tildy, to my great surprise, squeezed herself between me and the steering wheel where she sat tense and uncertain. As I murmured comfortingly to her, she licked my chin. Mary, as excited as I have ever seen her, was just longing to be back on the island. 'You're honoured,' she smiled, flicking a shadowy finger towards me, 'and I'm honoured too,' she went on, 'for I really feel that I'm heading for home.'

The night was ink black, the boat lurched to and fro and heavy waves smashed against the windscreen of the car and ran down it in rivulets. 'This is a good testing experience for you,' I called out, 'though I must warn you that it can be worse.' I glanced at her sideways though I could only see her dark form. One of my reasons for having suggested that she visited me during the winter months was to test her endurance of this kind of thing. 'You're really keen, aren't you?' I added. 'I can feel it.'

She laughed. 'It would take a great deal more than a rough sea to stop me now,' was her reply.

The journey that evening seemed never-ending and the thought that Rosemary would have a meal waiting for us, and a warm house, was a pleasant one.

'Surely we must be nearly there?' I queried aloud, after what seemed an interminable length of time. At that moment, the engines of the boat changed into a droning gear and the deck lights flickered on. 'The vessel seems to be doing much more twirling around than usual,' I commented. However, at that point it suddenly steadied and straightened on to a slow, even course. 'A few more minutes and we'll be in,' I yelled again, reassuringly. We waited for the sudden lurch forward as we docked and for the ramp to go down, and were not a little mystified when it did not happen. 'Actually, we've speeded up again . . . Yes, we're going far too fast to dock now, Mary, and listen, the engines have changed up! Wait a minute, d'you know I do believe that we're on our way back to Yell.' Moving Tildy over on to Mary's knee I heaved myself up in my seat as the deck lights blinked out, and caught a glimmer of the Fetlar terminal lights receding into the gloom. 'Oh my, it was obviously too rough to dock on,' I confirmed. 'Which means that this wind must be right into the west.'

'What on earth are we going to do?' Mary cried out.

'Don't worry, we'll be all right and this'll be a good lesson to you as to why Fetlar folk always have friends on Yell! There's two lots of people that spring to mind immediately. Alma and Dennis would certainly take us in if they're at home. Though I think we'll try someone a little nearer first.'

We arrived back at Yell feeling dog-tired, and to put the tin lid on the evening's events I caught our rusty old exhaust pipe on the ridge of the ramp as we came over it. The pipe snapped and we arrived at the home of my friends Brian and Irene sounding like a traction engine.

Brian and Irene lived near the ferry and permanently kept a twin-bedded room ready for such an emergency. Bless them, they welcomed us with open arms, showed us the facilities and said that supper would be ready in five minutes. They also told us that as soon as supper was over they would be going off to a carol service. 'Would you like to come with us?' Irene invited.

We glanced at each other surprised, then realised, silently, that it could not possibly be the bishop's carol service, which by that time would long have finished. We nodded our agreement as Irene put us more in the picture by mentioning the name of Magnus the minister, and that it was to be held over at the Presbyterian kirk at the north end of Yell.

Mary went off to the bathroom to freshen herself up and I looked around the comfortable room that we were to share. It was years since I had had to share a room with anyone else and I felt terribly shy.

We needed more hosts in the tabernacle at home in order to be able to make our Communions, and having been given the great privilege of carrying the Reserved Sacrament back from the church of St Magnus to Fetlar, I looked around for a safe nook where I could house it for the night. Having found one I unpacked my sponge bag and the few things that I would need.

'Oh dear,' whispered Mary as she re-entered. 'Sister, d'you know what? I've stupidly mislaid a bag, and not only does it contain my washing things but also, and more importantly, my Christmas gifts for you and Rosemary.'

'Oh dear . . . would you like me to look? What about the car?' I asked.

'No, I've looked there and I've thought and thought . . . and my conclusion is, that I left it where we changed cars with the Bishop.'

'Oh no . . . about twenty miles away,' I murmured. 'It'll be a bit wet by now.'

Later, over supper, having explained the situation to Brian and Irene, we took their advice and rang up the shop that was in the vicinity.

'Yes, it's there,' said the shopkeeper at once, 'and we brought it in out of the rain two hours ago. I'll send it over to the Fetlar ferry on the overland bus in the morning . . . No, no, it's all right, no trouble at all. Goodnight.'

Immediately after supper we zoomed off to the service, by which time it was snowing heavily. Afterwards, back at Irene's and Brian's we all had a cosy chat over our night drinks and went to bed. Mary and I said Compline quietly together in our room and thanked God for our safety and our wonderful friends.

Staggeringly, and in no time at all, Mary and Tildy the dog were both sound asleep and snoring in harmony. Being over-tired, sleep completely eluded me and I lay awake the whole night, happily content and conscious of the presence and peace of our Lord in the Sacrament. In his nearness I thanked him for blessings without number and asked for his continual loving aid to us all and all those whom we loved. Presently the volume from the other side of the room increased and I, surprisingly, enjoyed the nearness of the two snorers. 'This is my family making all this noise,' I suddenly thought, 'and how happy I am.'

The byre/chapel has always had a special feel to it. In fact, from the moment when I first peered through its rough door on the day that I arrived to live at The Ness, I knew that I had to make it our place of worship.

Today, almost eight years later, I'm sitting in one of the humblest choir stalls that you could imagine yet enjoying the fragrance of the many prayers which have been uttered here. We now have the Blessed Sacrament reserved on the altar in this area of the byre, an area we call our Lady Chapel. It's the place in which we say the Divine Office during the colder months of the year, for recently we've had, reluctantly, to convert the oratory in the house into a bedroom. Therefore this area, which can be sealed off just enough to keep out the worst of the draughts, has taken its place.

Three lamps are lit on ledges around me and are flickering long gleams across the stone walls and up and along the the wooden rafters of the roof.

In the silence the only sounds to be heard are those of the splutterings of our ancient gas heater, the gentle snoring of Tildy, our dog, and the munchings of the three occupants who are bedded down in the cattle stalls at the back of the building: Iona, the Golden Guernsey goat and the two kiddy lambs, Ramling and Foula.

A wooden prayer rail is fixed before me and moving forward I've knelt, leaned my elbows upon it and cupped my head into my hands. I try now to persuade all exterior things, all thoughts and feelings, to fall away and slowly, one by one, they're dispersing . . . until all that is left is that hard stubborn core of myself. I wait expectantly, for I'm not unversed in such prayer . . . Yes, it's as though God himself reaches down . . . so low, that with the tiniest thrust I'm loosened from the imprisonment of self and am in his arms where I belong, safe yet free, no longer the mistress of myself. Like a little one, like a bird, my soul's set free. Free to commune, to enjoy, to be cherished by God. Like my lark I'm held aloft where I can hover and pour out my song; the song of my love. Yet in it, embrace the world.

> The more thou thine own self
> Out of thyself dost throw
> The more will into thee
> God with his Godhead flow.[1]

6 Flying into the Wind

Christmas with Mary that year was a very special one and it came and went all too quickly. One of the loveliest things that I remember about it was a sharing of classical music. I had a small, cheap cassette player and over the holiday period we listened to a great deal of Elgar and Greig. Greig somehow, for me, perfectly catches the spirit of the north and not only of his own northern country but that also of Shetland. We listened to his Piano Concerto in A minor several times during that week and suddenly I was able to admit to my new friend that years before I had had a great urge to be able to write poetry in the same manner as he had written his music.

So, unable to hold them back, the last joyful days of that year came to an end and I accompanied Mary back to Lerwick to see her off. This was quite something for me, since I rarely left the island, and only then if there was some really urgent reason for doing so.

We arrived in the town before lunch and after we had had a bite to eat she suggested, no, insisted, that with the little money that she had left from her visit to Shetland, we hire a car for a couple of hours.

'Hire a car?' I asked, wondering if I'd heard aright.

'Oh, do say yes, and then we can go off and find those wool mills.'

'Wool mills?'

'Yes, you know, that advert I read out to you the other day, when you wondered if they'd have some suitable Shetland tweed to make yourself a winter habit. Come on, let's go and see . . . They might just have enough to make me one too,' she winked.

Having done this and found that the mill was closed, we decided that since we had the car at our disposal and were so near to St Ninian's Isle, a small islet soaked in Celtic and Viking history, we would head in that direction. Tildy would love it, we knew, as indeed she did, and to each of us the place was as yet only a name.

St Ninian's Isle is joined by a narrow isthmus to the south-west Mainland and is a strand so beautiful that many, Father Lewis, included, think of it as *the* beauty spot of Shetland. We arrived in the sunshine and spent almost an hour walking quietly across its solitary beach. We were enthralled by the spectrum of colour, for neither of us had ever realised how many variations of blue and greens there can be and how enhanced they can be by dunes and the rock-pooled sand. Seeing and sharing such beauty at a time which was so poignant in our lives, made this place then, and still, a special place to us.

'Now, what about Easter?' asked Mary later, as we said our final farewell in. Lerwick. 'Could you cope with me for yet another holiday?'

'Yes, I'd love you to come, though . . .'

'I'll have to save up very hard of course, and actually, it'll be the last time before my permanent arrival in July . . .'

'Yes,' I said when I eventually got a word in, 'actually I've been wondering about all of that myself and I just might have a better suggestion to make. You see, I was fairly certain you'd ask to come up for Easter, and putting it alongside the fact that Rosemary's been bullying me, as she does every two years or so, to take another holiday, I think that I've come up with an idea that'll please you. What I have in mind is, that instead of your coming up to Shetland, why don't I meet you in Aberdeen and we'll go to Iona, not for the actual festival but for the week immediately afterwards?'

'Wow! Yes please, I'd love to. Are you serious?'

'Of course I'm serious. You love that area and I've waited thirteen years for the right moment when I might return, so why don't we? Iona, as you know, is the place where I received my call to come north, and strangely enough, I knew then, all those years ago, that the next time I sailed in her direction God's promises concerning SOLI would have been accomplished. They have, a hundredfold, and I think that now it would be nice for you and me to go back there together and say thank you . . . And perhaps, together, dig a little more of the foundations upon which the community is to be built. What do you think?'

'Absolutely super! I can't wait,' she beamed. 'Though, just a minute – isn't Frances hoping to come up to The Ness for the Easter break? Rosemary's there I know, yet we can't really go off and leave them, can we? Not when Frances is coming up specially to see you. She'd be terribly disappointed.'

'No, we most certainly can't. I'd better write and ask her exactly what her plans are before we arrange anything further. She could always come up and spend the first week of her fortnight with me and then stay on and help Rosemary look after things whilst I'm away. Does she drive, d'you know? Because that could be really useful to Rosemary, and also she could stay in The Ness rather than in the caravan and look after the cats. There'd be someone actually in the house then to give them lots of tender loving care.'

We said our goodbyes and I clambered on to the overland bus that would take me as far as Yell. 'See you at Easter!' I waved, and this time my eyes were a little damp as the bus pulled away. She, giving a final wave back, made her way to the ship with the ever-exuberant Tildy at her heels.

Frances was delighted with the idea of spending a week with me at The Ness and then cat-sitting along with Rosemary. 'Please, though,' she begged, 'could there be some time before you go off, to talk to you about my retirement plans?'

January was a wild month and during the latter half I made ready for Rose's return for a fortnight. As with Mary Father Lewis had thought that it would be a good idea if she came up to stay during the winter to see if she could stand the bleakness of the season as well as the short dark days and the long, even darker, nights.

This time, when we went to meet Rose at the ferry she was actually on deck and waving as the boat drew in. It was a joy to see her again and we rushed her home to give her something warm to eat and drink. Being an Australian she found the climate something of a shock, though over her stay she adjusted marvellously. The caravans were far too flimsy, of course, to sleep in at this time of the year, so I had turned the ben room into a bed-sitter for her. There, we had some huge peat fires which were wonderful to sit and talk by in the evenings, often along with Rosemary.

Rose's call to Fetlar was puzzling to me for she was a very able and dedicated nurse. From the time of her childhood in Australia all she had ever wanted was to nurse and latterly, until God had beckoned her in the direction of Fetlar, her great desire had been to specialise seriously in hospice work. Being of the mind that if the Lord gives us a gift it should be used, I was therefore in a quandary. For how could SOLI, at least my vision of SOLI, and hospice nursing, come together? In fact, it was not until a week or so after she had returned to Sussex that the answer came to me.

However, during her visit we walked and talked and on a cold winter's morning during her stay, headed in the direction of Strandibrough, an ancient monastery site which lies on an eastern peninsula of the isle. Having to make the most of the daylight hours, I decided that we had best go by car as far as the road would take us and then trek over the moorland by the edge of the sea. It was a bitterly cold day and having arrived we did not take too long to eat our lunch. Perched there on the promontory, I told Rose the little I knew of the place, adding that I had never been sure whether the boulders lying around and sticking up here and there were supposed to be the remains of a Viking or a Celtic monastery. Clouds scudded across the sky and as time ticked by, grew more and more ominous-looking. Getting the message, we quickly stuffed the remains of our picnic into our bags and headed for home. We talked much of spiritual matters as we strode along, ascertaining amongst other things that we were in sympathy over such aspects as simplicity, poverty and freedom. Gusts of the rising wind became increasingly fierce. So fierce, that we could hardly walk against them and had to cease talking. However, we thrust forward, and what a relief it was to reach the car. Rose, the same middling height as I, slightly slimmer and certainly a few years younger, was as worn out with the effort as her guide.

We found Rosemary up at The Ness when we arrived home, looking alarmed. 'Thank goodness you're back,' she sighed with relief. 'An unexpected force 11 gale's been forecast, I heard it over lunch and it's due to hit Shetland this afternoon. By the way,' she went on, 'did you notice the barn roof as you passed it?'

'Tell us the worst,' I groaned.

'Ah yes, well, I noticed it about an hour ago, through the window . . . A corner of the felt is flapping like mad.'

I tore out to look and realised that unless we did something about it, and at once, the whole roof would be ripped to shreds. 'Rose,' I called, 'could you come and give me a hand quickly? And Rosemary, did you say that you had a tin of five-inch nails?'

Rosemary went off to look for the nails in her barn, whilst Rose hastily gathered up some long planks of wood. Quickly, rushing back into the house, I pulled on some old working clothes and dashed out again. Then, slipping into our own barn, I collected together a ladder, my biggest hammer and a motley collection of secondhand nails. Rose was marvellous. As I nailed the planks across the roof as quickly as I could, she, from the ladder, held one of my feet to a foothold and passed up whatever I needed. Holding on to the roof almost with gritted teeth, I slipped and twisted in the blasts, hoping that I could stay the course. Each time that Rose needed to step off the ladder, which occasionally she did, I simply stopped working and concentrated my whole attention on clinging to the roof. Each time that she stepped from the ladder, either to move it on, or to collect another fistful of nails, it instantly blew over and had to be re-erected. After an hour of this kind of buffeting we could hardly see, for by then it was dark. Nevertheless by that time we had secured the felting enough for it to withstand the gale. Trembling, I clambered down, thinking that tomorrow we would see how hideous it all looked, though at least we could sleep in peace knowing that the roof was safe. Thankfully we tidied up and went in to drink a hot cup of tea made by Rosemary and to wash off the grime and dirt in preparation for Vespers.

Rose thoroughly enjoyed her stay, though there was still the slight niggle of a doubt in her mind as to whether the religious life was really for her. She wanted desperately to believe that it was, yet the question mark about order and corporate, formalised worship, dogged her evangelical heart.

Due mostly to the weather, we were well into the spring before Father Lewis managed to get out to Fetlar to say Mass for Rosemary and me and to have a proper catch-up on news. On this occasion, because time was so limited between ferries, Rosemary kindly offered to wash up the lunch dishes whilst Father and I did the talking. So, sitting in front of the ben room fire that we had made for the occasion I brought him up to date with all our doings.

'Father, what are we going to do about accommodation when Mary and Rose arrive?' I concluded.

'Mary actually arrives in three months, does she?' he asked.

'Yes, she'll have to have this room with the bed in the corner. She and Rose both used it happily when they came up for their winter visits. It's a dark old room, though cheery with a fire, and we'll just need to use the but room as a sitting-room as well as to eat in. At the moment, I haven't the heart to dismantle the oratory.'

The oratory was the tiny loft room chapel which I had used along with Rosemary before the byre/chapel was converted. Indeed, we have only recently stopped using it, having now moved into the Lady Chapel for our winter Offices. The oratory, dedicated to Jesus the Good Shepherd, with its white sloping walls, its distinctive atmosphere and its altar, was a darling little place, unspeakably special.

'I think,' Father said hesitantly, 'that you'll need to turn it into a bedroom for Rose. A shame, but there's nothing else for it. Presumably there's still no possibility of your landlord selling you the house, is there? Because, of course, the ideal thing would be to build a room or two on to it.'

'No, absolutely none at the moment,' I told him. 'It's a great pity, for I've always known that it has great potential and its market value, I suspect, would be quite low . . . It's a very special place to me too, and I'm sure we could have raised two or three thousand, albeit out of a hat, had the opportunity arisen. And yes, you're right, Father, we could have built on to it in a very simple way and still retained its character. However, there's no chance and there's no other property that's feasible on Fetlar.' I told him about my ideas of Brough Lodge being happily dissolved and he stared into the fire, his brow furrowed for a while.

'Mmm, I'm glad that Brough didn't come to anything.' He smiled. He is younger than I by as much as twelve years and although knowing this (I, at this time, was in my mid-forties), I respected the wisdom that went with his few already greying hairs. A piece of salty driftwood flared and spattered up the chimney and he turned towards me, his eyes gleaming. 'I know,' he challenged. 'What about building?'

'Oh no, Father, not build, I really don't want to build, and however are we to find enough money to build anyway, with only two hundred pounds in the bank and nothing but the odd surprise donation coming in?'

'Sister, what have you just said to me about buying The Ness? Was it something about raising money out of a hat? Come on . . . you know as well as I do that if you're meant to build, the money will come. And look,' he said, seeing my immediate reluctance, 'look, you like this area, you're well established in it, so why don't you ask Andrew and Sheila if they'll sell you a piece of land? It seems perhaps a ridiculous idea, but do write to them and let's see what opens up.'

Andrew and his wife Sheila, who own the land around The Ness, are good friends of ours and during the early years of their marriage had lived in Lower Ness. In fact it was this couple from whom Rosemary had bought the house in 1984. However, since that time they had moved from their new home on Fetlar to live on the Shetland Mainland and we had kept an eye on the flock of sheep that they had left behind.

Since Father Lewis had suggested that I write to them and as I do not believe in hanging around about such things, the next day I sat down and did so. Was there any possible chance, I asked, of purchasing enough ground upon which to build a house and chapel out on The Ness headland? Three weeks later, when to be quite honest I had almost forgotten that I had communicated, Andrew drew up in his Landrover outside The Ness.

Everything was grey that day, the sea, the sky and my mood. It was one of those occasions when things go wrong and the final straw had been that I was going to be late for the kirk. Throwing my cloak around my shoulders I unlatched the garden gate and sped through it. At that moment I saw them.

'I've caught you at an awkward moment, I can see,' called Andrew.

'No, no, do come in.'

'We're going up to look at the sheep on the hill with a few of the other crofters, and we're booked out on the evening ferry, so thanks a lot, Sister, but we won't come in this time. Anyhow, what we're wanting to say really won't take more than a couple of seconds . . . First of all, my apologies for not having answered your letter. The reason was that I needed to go and talk with the Crofting Commissioners and ask their advice with regard to the piece of land that you're wanting to buy from us.'

'Oh, Andrew, how exciting . . .'

'Primarily, I went along to see them because there were one or two queries that needed to be ironed out.' He went on to explain to me what the problems had been and how they were to be resolved. Then, to my astonishment, he added that since he now knew where he stood legally, not only was there a piece of land available but that he and Sheila would like to *give* it to me. I was utterly speechless, though in the end managed to burble something that sounded like 'Thank you'.

Andrew smiled. 'I'm no Christian, but if you build over there,' and he pointed to exactly the spot that I had in mind, 'if you build over there you'll certainly be building on rock.'

The Ness garden is one of the few places on Fetlar where bluebells grow in great profusion, and although the family, especially Sister Mary Clare, try every so often to persuade me to have a blitz on them, to dig most of them up and to make room for a whole galaxy of other flowers, I can't bring myself to the point of doing it.

I'm sitting on the little lawn surrounded by them now, and how uplifting they are. Beyond their bobbing heads is our dry-stone garden dyke and beyond that, another blue drift of sea and sky. Blues and greens, along with an oatmeal-coloured habit, are our colours. So how well we are camouflaged into our habitat, especially at this time of the year. No, these darling flowers represent to me something of the nature of our life here, of its wild simple beauty and sturdiness and its resilience against the elements.

On my own and then with Rosemary, God protected and nurtured us and we multiplied and became a community. Now, hundreds of people know of SOLI, throughout Britain and further afield. We are appreciated and given help. Andrew and Sheila gave me land. Kind benefactors have sent food parcels, warm clothes and donations, so that now we are not as poor or struggling. Yet, this is where we have to be careful. Careful not to sit back on our laurels and think how wonderful we are. No, we have to hold on to the simple natural ways of God and never in our hearts stop depending upon him. Of course there is nothing wrong with extra colour being added to our lives to give it contrast and balance, or with the acceptance of loving help from various sources. It's just that, 'Please God, let us never replace the love of ourselves or the world, for you.'

> *Be the dust ne'er so vile, be the motes*
> *ne'er so small,*
> *The wise man sees God, great and*
> *glorious, in them all.*[1]

7 Glimpsed through the Rainbow

Rosemary had not been able to go to the kirk on that particular Sunday when Andrew and Sheila imparted to me the wonderful tidings about the land. So quickly, unable to contain myself a second longer, I helter-skeltered down to Lower Ness to tell her the news. She was as elated with it as I was – and I, not surprisingly, was very late for the service! Later, we talked and talked of what we could build, and many a croft house was built in the air!

Although Mary and I had arranged to go to Iona immediately after Easter, she decided in the end to come up to Shetland first and celebrate the festival with us. So, arriving in time for the Holy Week ceremonies, she had her first taste of Anglo-Catholicism in full swing. 'Not my cup of tea,' she confessed months later during one of our stimulating discussions over churchmanship. Nevertheless, her preferences did not spoil this holy season of the Church's year for any of us. For myself, I suspected that God was having a little joke with me by sending such an Evangelical aspirant.

Because of responsibilities in his own churches over the great festivals of Easter and Christmas, Father Lewis has never managed to come over to Fetlar at these times. Partly of course, this has been due to the long travelling distances involved, for we are approximately sixty miles and two ferry trips from Lerwick. However, I have always managed the services, in as far as I could without a priest. So that with regard to Holy Week the Paschal Proclamation and the Litanies have been sung and a Paschal Candle has been lit. Also, since the bishop marvellously allowed me to have the reserved Sacrament when I first came here, we are privileged to be able to make our Communion on great feasts and sometimes on Sundays.

Now Frances was not, as they say, 'at the bottom of the

candle' with regard to church ritual, and would have given a great deal to join us for Holy Week and Easter. However, being an organist at a local church near her home, she could not manage to get away until Easter Monday and so did not arrive on Fetlar until the Tuesday. After that, a few days were spent over her first week on the island when we familiarised her with her animal charges and allowed them plenty of time to get used to her. Frances is a gentle, fun-loving soul, so it soon became apparent that she and my horde were going to have a joyful time.

During our few days together, we made time in which we could talk and discussed seriously the possibility of her becoming an Associate member of SOLI. Although I had been aware of her interest in joining us, I had not anticipated her wishing to do so at so deep a level of commitment. So I was delighted when she divulged that she was seriously thinking of asking me if she might come and live alongside us in the same way that Rosemary had, when she retired the following year. However, at that point we decided that we would go on thinking about it and make the appropriate plans when she came up to Fetlar during the summer holidays.

Full of excitement I began to pack for my second visit to Iona. It was, too, only the second holiday that I had had during my five years on Fetlar, so I was in real need of a rest and change. However, when the time came for our departure it was not without great sadness, for I hated leaving my two friends, my little animal family and the home that I loved. Mary carried me along on the crest of her enthusiasm, quickly bundling my suitcase into the car, and me too, slamming the door and jumping in herself before I could change my mind.

Rosemary and Frances took us to the ferry and saw us off. Slowly, their waving figures receded into the blur that was Fetlar. Turning to Mary, I smiled and it was then, unexpectedly, that I recovered my pleasurable glow which filtered through me despite the cold wind and rain.

Later that day, having reached Lerwick, we boarded the St Clair. There, we were immediately taken along to our double cabin by a steward and were not a little disappointed to

discover that it was an inner one. Some folk find these claustrophobic, though for myself, if I am allotted this type of cabin,
without a porthole, I simply go off to bed early. 'Oh well,' I
lamented, throwing my luggage on to the higher bunk, 'we'll
be sleeping most of the time anyway, so why make a fuss?'

'You go away so rarely though,' protested Mary. 'It would
have been nice for you to have had a porthole . . . Hold on a
second, I've an idea. Don't start unpacking yet.' She took my
arm, steered me out of the door and in a trice had me standing
in front of the purser. To my astonishment she then, over my
shoulder, asked if it were at all possible to have a cabin with a
porthole.

'Yes, I think that might be possible,' he said, smiling at me in
a quizzical manner and running his finger down the passenger
list. 'Hi John,' he beckoned a second steward, 'would you
mind moving these two ladies over the passage?' Keys jangled
between them and in no time at all we were esconced in a
pleasant cabin for two streaming with light. Peering together
through the porthole we watched Lerwick disappearing
beyond sight.

After our fourteen-hour voyage we awoke in Aberdeen to a
beautiful sunny day and decided, as a special holiday treat,
that we would breakfast on the ship before disembarking.
Indeed, by the time that the meal was called we were as much
in need of the relaxation as of the food. We had just spent a
solid half hour frantically searching for Mary's spectacles in
every nook of the cabin. She swore that I had scooped them up
into the bedclothes that I had folded, and that they were
smashed and that she would never be able to see properly
again, and for the first time I realised that her grannie must
have had red hair! Finally, when in her mind she had cancelled
our trip to Iona because she would not be able to see to drive,
we discovered them over the passage in the shower room/
toilet and all was well.

Breakfast over, we rose reconciled, happy and all set for our
long journey to Oban. Mary had left her car waiting for us in
Aberdeen, so within an hour of docking we were *en route* for
Iona. What a wonderful new store of memories that journey

gave us, stopping here and there for a cup of coffee, admiring the lovely picturesque scenery and then having a break for a fish-and-chip lunch in a friendly town. We arrived in Oban with only half an hour to spare and immediately boarded the car ferry for Mull.

Once settled on board, memories crowded my mind. Instantly, I was transported back to the 20th October, 1978 when Rosemary and I had returned from her third and my first holiday on Iona. The engines of the vessel had roared into action and the vibration of the throbbing engines had seemed to be telling me as we moved away from the Isles that the next time I heard them on this same passage the call that had been given me on Iona would be in part fulfilled. That prophecy had come true and there were no words that could express the overflowing of my heart.

Soon, Mull was sighted and we rolled off the ferry and began our long-awaited, and my long-imagined, drive across the island. So many times since 1976 I had relived that journey, and on this particular day as the mountains grew higher and the sky grew more ominous and stormy-looking, I thanked God for the perfecting of his will.

'Sister, do you mind if I stop, just for a moment to take a quick photo?' asked Mary.

'Of course not, I've heard this before,' I answered. 'Please do.'

'It's only that there's a gorgeous rainbow . . . Look over there.'

I looked, wondering if I could contain yet more joy. Yes, there it was, the most glorious rainbow that I had ever seen. My heart thrilled, for since that first trip here, rainbows had featured in my life as a great sign of hope, and now this one! I though, 'What an affirmation of the glory and the love of God it is.' We jumped out of the car, took two photographs and then sped on our way. 'Though this time, dear Lord,' I said, and spoke with no sound, 'we're not on any account going to miss our boat to the "Isle of Glory".'

Tired and triumphant we landed on Iona and no, we did *not* miss the boat as Rosemary and I had done in 1976. Our landlady gave us a marvellous welcome, a cup of tea and something to eat and we relaxed and enjoyed her company. She also gave us something more than just friendship and food, something which we have long afterwards remembered, and it happened like this. During our conversation with her, she suddenly paused and looked penetratingly across at each of us, first at one and then at the other, and then laughingly asked if we were by any chance related. We teasingly asked why she thought that we might be, and she answered at once, 'Because,' she said, 'you have the same eyes.'

'Green eyes?' we asked.

'No, not quite,' she murmured still staring intensely.

'Happy eyes?' we ventured.

'No, almost . . . Yes . . . No, it's your *joyful* eyes,' she declared.

We both twinkled at each other, thinking what a wonderful compliment it was.

'Yes, well, we're almost Sisters!' I explained.

What a delightfully happy holiday we had. Having booked our landlady's tiny self-catering bungalow, which she called her 'backhouse', we were independent and this suited us marvellously for we could come and go as we pleased.

During that time there, Mary and I learned to understand each other at a much deeper level, perceiving not only the surface niceties that everyone knows and sees, but also the more prickly bits underneath that have to be lived with, and then through them, down to the deep things that the soul is made of. Yes, our time together was invaluable and we came out at the end of it still wanting to found SOLI!

One of the great highlights for me was the visiting of Greenbank. This was the house where Rosemary and I had stayed thirteen years previously. Now it had become an important place in our community history since it was, virtually, where the community had been born. Mollie, who had lived there and looked after us so marvellously, had moved to Oban, having sold the house to a very nice retired lady doctor. Nancy, the new owner, invited us for tea and gave us a conducted tour around the little house. What a wonderful pleasure it was to find, in one of the bedrooms, sitting exactly where I had put it on the shelf, the tiny triptych that I had left behind as a token of my call. Nancy had in fact written to me, having read *A Tide that Sings*, introducing herself and telling me that it was still there.

After Nancy's super tea we walked on Traighmor, the beach in front of the house where I had sat on my last morning there in 1976, making great decisions.

Here I could write screeds on the beauty, the spirituality and the new memories that have been stored by us of Iona. Yet for now, I must pass on, though with the promise of a return.

As Mary had to be back at school by a certain date, after ten days on Iona we had reluctantly to think of our departure. Indeed, we had already extended our stay by two days and could not financially afford longer.

As we had the car and as Mary wanted me to visit her parents and I wanted to visit my sister Carole, I travelled with her as far as Worcester, where I stayed in the boarding house of Mary's school for three nights. From there we visited various friends, two of whom I must mention, for although they do not feature in the story of this book in a physical way they have for many years been a powerful spiritual support to me. They are Anne and Joyce, now resident in an Oxfordshire nursing home and to whom I owe my deepest love and thanks. Marvellously, too, I was privileged not only to be able to introduce Mary to them but also Rose. We found that their place of abode was as accessible to Rose as it was to us, thus it provided us with a lovely halfway meeting place.

Noticing that Rose looked wan when we first met jolted me into having a few private words with her. Sadly, she had continued to have doubts with regard to attaching herself to a religious community, and wondered how I would feel about putting our arrangement on to hold, at least for the moment. This I agreed to, with sadness, though I hope with sense.

Saying goodbye to Mary was hard, though as she said as we heaved my suitcase into the train, the next time that we would meet was only two and a half months away, and that would be for keeps.

On my journey back to Fetlar I stayed with Carole my sister. This was a great delight, for although we are not often in touch by letter we are in fact close and it was a tremendous joy to me to see her. She and Eric, her husband, had been married in Shetland only two years previously and this has made an even stronger link. Rosemary and I had stood as their witnesses and were teasingly described by Carole as her 'bridesmaids'. Eric, a gentle and dear brother-in-law, is a Yorkshire man and as proud of it as Rosemary is of being a Yorkshire woman. These two became great friends, with the result that Eric insisted that Rosemary was to be his 'best man'. She agreed wholeheartedly and did the job well. We all howled with laughter when Eric decided to give her a kiss of thanks after the service at St Colman's church, announcing as he did so that that was the first time he'd ever kissed his best man! I was delighted to visit their home in south Yorkshire for the first time and to find to my surprise that they had called it Burravoe after the place on Yell where they had been married.

After one other short pause in North Yorkshire with Rosemary's sister and brother-in-law who are Caim members of SOLI, I made tracks at long last for home . . .

What a joy it was to get back to Shetland, from where by then Frances had departed, though what a welcome home Rosemary and the pussies gave me.

'Are you sure that you've got all you'll need, Sister? I could easily post things on to you.'

'Sister Mary Clare, you've inundated me with all I'll ever want and more, so the answer is, Yes, I've got all I need and no, I don't want anything else sent on. Thank you and bless you.'

Having flung our arms around each other in a final embrace, we've loaded my two bags on to the boat, helped by a crew member who is standing below, and now I must myself clamber over the side. There is quite a drop into the vessel and as I step tentatively down a vertical ladder, I feel a wave of secret excitement wafting over me. This is

*exactly how I felt on each of those occasions when I visited Iona,
though this time it is a different isle; it is the isle of Papa Stour. This
isle is on the west side of Shetland and it's my first visit; the special
reason being to finish the manuscript for this book. Life is busy at
home at the moment, so my very thoughtful community have suggested that I step aside for at least a week, and have time to think.
'You need to get right away,' they insisted, 'away from your duties,
distractions and the telephone.' Since I have not managed to have a
holiday for eighteen months or so, and there is nothing I would rather
do more than spend a week or ten days writing, I was easily persuaded. Though actually, I am so happy on Fetlar that when it comes
to the point of leaving it even for a holiday, it's usually with reluctance. However this time, to my surprise, having got the 'Iona feel',
it's not!*

*Wild flurries of snow hit us as we drove over the Mainland to this
remote little ferry terminal. Now, as the clouds break up, the odd
desultory snowflake still floats on to the bleak February scene.*

*'Don't wait out here in this bitter cold. Go and sit in the car,
Sister,' I call up to her, partly because I'm feeling so perished myself
and selfishly would like to get out of the icy blast. 'There's another
ten minutes at least before we leave.'*

*Looking down from the edge of the pier she's laughing. 'Would you
do that, if you were seeing me off?'*

*'No,' I demur and, duly put in my place, grin back . . . Now I'll
need to brace myself and stick it out until we sail. As I do so, I realise
afresh, as I have on so many occasions, that I will greatly miss her.
'We'll come together next time,' I promise.*

*The sky has an ominous look as cloud formations speed across it,
and something of the 'Iona feel' catches me again. Waving my arm in
an arc I can't help but intimate that . . . 'All we need now is our
rainbow.'*

'Yes.' Her eyes sweep the heavens and she smiles.

*Our final parting is to be abrupt, for suddenly, shuddering into
life, the rust-pitted twelve-seater tub has twisted from its moorings
and is plunging forth into the open sea. Snow is falling heavily now,
and Sister Mary Clare standing at the pier head, a solitary figure,
waves until she is no more than the size of a pin-prick. At last,
brushing the flakes from my sleeves, I step into the cabin.*

As I've said, at each juncture on my spiritual journey – that is, since God called me to these Northern Isles – there's always been a rainbow! 'What a coincidence' I can hear you say. Yet, coincidence or not, it is true for me that a rainbow does seem to mark significant events. So true is this that I now automatically look around for this symbol of what I think of as confirmative love. As the lark trills out her song of this same love, so this arc of colour speaks to me of the essence of life.

The crossing, which takes about half an hour, is noted for being atrocious and I, not having realised this, am completely unprepared for the violent attack of nausea that's just hit me. Thankfully, apart from the crewmen who are out in front, I'm the only passenger; even so, I pray that I may manage to retain my dignity. Sitting as close as I can to the narrowest door that I've ever seen in my life that is marked 'Toilet', I've just looked at my watch to find that there's at least another fifteen minutes to go. Suddenly I've remembered some long-ago advice for controlling faintness by putting one's head between one's knees. Sickness and faintness are different, of course, though at this moment anything's worth a try. Bending forward I've closed my eyes and slowly, slowly, to my astonishment I feel better. Time now accelerates . . . and here we are bumping up against the island pier. Our two friends are waiting. Andy's taking my luggage and carrying it over to their tractor and trailer on which we're to travel. Sabina's helping me from the boat. Standing upright on terra firma I greet her and take stock . . . There, arched over her shoulder, is a rainbow!

8 *Wheels of Flight*

Rose had also arranged for herself a week on Iona, though a few weeks after us, over the Whitsun holiday. Happily, whilst she was there, some of her uncertainties about coming to Fetlar were sorted out. Subsequently I received a treasured missive asking if she might, after all, join us.

On the same day that Rose's letter arrived there was in the post a small brown paper parcel. Opening it I found a couple of slim paperbacks about Cornish churches. Tucked into one of them was a letter from the gentleman who, with his wife, had written and illustrated them. He said that he had bought and read my book, *A Tide that Sings*, and had so enjoyed it that he was sending me copies of theirs. Knowing and loving Cornwall from the many holidays that I had spent there over the twenty-one years that I had lived in Devon, made the books a special gift. So I wrote back almost at once to thank Roger and his wife Esther, and with my letter I enclosed our latest newsletter, in which I told of the wonderful gift of land that we had been given. Almost by return of post he wrote back to me saying that he was an architect and if ever we needed his services he would give them freely!

'Marvellous,' I exclaimed to myself as I read the last few sentences. 'First we're given a gift of land and now an architect is offering us his help. We must be on the right track. I'd better ring Lewis.'

It was during this time, the spring of 1989, that I received an unexpected late-night telephone call. In actual fact Mary herself had promised to ring on that particular evening and had apologised that it would be late rather than early. So at quarter past ten, seated in my dressing gown by the fire, I was sipping my night drink and waiting for the phone to ring. 'Hello,' I said cheerily, when it did, without properly announcing myself, which is something I rarely do.

'Good evening, is that Sister Agnes?' said a deep voice in reply.

Taken aback, I apologised for sounding so casual and asked if I could help.

'You may well be able to, Sister. I'm ringing on behalf of Grampion Television . . .'

'Oh,' I groaned not able to keep the dismay out of my voice.

'That doesn't sound a very helpful response,' he laughed.

'No, I'm sorry. I'm not keen on being public . . .'

It appeared that my caller was a regional producer of Sir Harry Secombe's ITV *Highway* programme. Having just read *A Tide that Sings*, he wanted me to take part in the Shetland programme that was due to be filmed at any moment. After he had persuasively talked over some of the ins and outs of it with me I weak-mindedly said yes, with the result that, since he was in Shetland, he came out to Fetlar and spent most of the next day discussing it further.

'We'll come and do at least half a day's filming here at The Ness,' he said, 'and then we'll need to take you into Lerwick for the actual interview. We'll do this, rather than having to charter another plane to bring out more of the crew and Sir Harry. Oh, and would you mind choosing a favourite reading with which we can end this particular series?'

Having cleared up all the imminent details, we then sat down to lunch and spent a jolly hour chatting of other things until it was time for him to go off for the ferry.

Before the film crew flew over to Fetlar, Alan, the producer, rang me twice more. The first time it was in a particularly excited manner. 'Sister, you know that I asked you to choose something to read at the end of your interview? Well, I don't know whether you've chosen anything yet, but I've just come across the Prayer of St Francis and feel that that would be absolutely ideal. Would you be willing? Oh yes, and the other thing is have you any particular preference with regard to location for your interview?'

'St Magnus, the Episcopalian church, would be a lovely place for the interview,' I suggested thinking that Father Lewis and some of our Anglican friends there might be rather pleased at the idea. 'And yes, I had actually chosen a reading, so I'm a bit disappointed, much as I love the prayer you suggest.'

During the evening before the cameras descended on The Ness, Father Lewis rang me. 'Sister, I've just heard a rumour that your interview's to be in the Presbyterian church instead of St Magnus . . .'

'Now, is that so, Father? Well, I'll see about that tomorrow,' I answered meaningfully.

The next morning, whilst cameras and lights were being strung up in the byre/chapel, my nice producer, his assistant and I sat around the but room table and discussed the proceedings.

'Now what about the final reading?' Alan concluded.

'Well,' I said, 'I've decided that I'll do the St Francis prayer as you've asked me to, though only on one condition and that is, that I'm interviewed in St Magnus' church.'

They both roared with laughter, 'Sister Agnes,' smiled Hilary the assistant producer, 'we can hardly say no to that, especially since we've already put the St Francis prayer in the script.'

When the day of the interview arrived, I was met at the ferry on the Shetland Mainland by an elderly, gentlemanly taxi driver who treated me as though I were royalty. En route to Lerwick, he remarked, 'Ah now, I've always wanted to meet Sir Harry, I'm a great fan of his. Always watch his programmes I do . . . yes, never miss.'

He dropped me at the Shetland Hotel, where I was given lunch and introduced to Sir Harry. After some happy chat, we were eventually collected in a royal-looking car and along with Ronnie Cass, the series producer, were driven through Lerwick. This was quite an experience for me and by this time I had to stop myself from waving gracefully out of the window.

However, we had some stimulating conversation en route, during which I asked the two men if by any chance they remembered a certain song which had been copyrighted for the *Highway* programme.

'Yes we do,' they replied unanimously, when I told them the title. 'Why do you ask?'

'Because the man who wrote the song is ailing and living for the day when you sing it on *Highway*. He's the uncle of a woman who is about to join me, that's how I know.'

To my astonishment, they not only knew the song and were able to tell me that it was to be sung in the very near future, but also told me a great deal more about the composer than I had learned from Mary, even to the fact that his wife was in hospital.

'It goes like this,' said Sir Harry, and sang it as we rode along.

Soon we reached the church, where special lighting was being set up and cameras being moved into place. Yes, all this had been transported from the Presbyterian kirk where some filming had actually already been done. It was to my shame, for how much easier I could have made life for them if I had been interviewed there. The fact was that I had had no idea how much work would be involved in the moving of all the equipment. As we walked in through the church doors, Father Lewis greeted us. Then we seemed to be carried along by a multitude of people. The building was crowded with human beings, cameras, wires and paraphernalia. Hilary greeted me and introduced me to some of the team that I had not already met. We chatted a while, and as we did so, I happened to notice a little way up the aisle Sir Harry having his face powdered by a make-up lady with an enormous powder puff. 'Do I have to have that done?' I asked incredulously.

'Yes,' laughed Hilary, 'it's to prevent the cameras catching the shine on your face.'

In due course Sir Harry and I were seated together in a front pew and after a nerve-racking count down had our six-minute interview. He asked me the first and what turned out to be the only question: What had made me come to live in Shetland, since I had been born and brought up in Nottingham? I need not have had any anxieties, for he was such an easy man to talk to and was so genuinely interested in what I was telling him that in fact words bubbled out, and he simply allowed me to talk. When it was over, I breathed a sigh of relief – that is, until Ronnie and Alan, who were kneeling on the floor with a whole lot of other people doing various jobs in front of us, suggested to Sir Harry that he did a few 'Yes, No's'!

'I don't think I can possibly go through all that again,' I said, startled.

'No, no, you don't need to,' replied Alan. 'Your part was fine. No, Sir Harry knows what I mean. All you need to do is sit and look at him. Are you ready, Sir Harry?'

Sir Harry was given another count down and then started saying, 'Mmm, yes, no, really, yes, I see, no . . .' He could see that I wanted to giggle and when it was over bent towards me and whispered with a chuckle, 'Don't you feel a twit?'

We sat and chatted then for another ten minutes or more, until someone patted me on the shoulder and reminded me that if I was intending to catch the last ferry I must depart immediately. Standing, I put out a hand to say goodbye, and to my pleasure Sir Harry gave me a friendly hug.

However, on my way out I was accosted by a photographer who wanted some photographs of Sir Harry and me at the church door. In two shakes we were posing in the doorway, laughing at Sir Harry's teasing thought that we would be able to say goodbye all over again!

Photographs taken, we found that the chauffeur had arrived and that, along with Ronnie, we were travelling back to the Shetland Hotel together. So there was a lovely bonus of a few more minutes of friendship in which we talked mostly on a spiritual topic.

At the hotel door my taxi driver was waiting. 'Sir Harry, could you spare a moment and would you mind,' I asked, 'greeting this elderly man? He happens to be a great fan of yours.'

Without the slightest hesitation this was done, and how thrilled my friend and his charming wife were. She was sitting in the cab watching. After farewells I returned to Fetlar, thankfully, though just a little bit walking on air! What a lovely person Sir Harry was! He had always been a favourite celebrity of my mother's, and I could not help thinking how thrilled she would have been.

During my last few weeks of living on my own, much

needed to be done, both physically and spiritually, in preparation for Mary's arrival. Rosemary was away south at her college reunion and doing her annual tour around her relatives and friends in England. So I was looking after Kelpie and the ducks for her, as well as coping with the visitors, callers, and trying to keep my work fitted within the framework of prayer and the Divine Office. The garden seemed to be growing more weeds than it had ever done before. All sorts of repair jobs suddenly needed to be seen to, including a rotten part of the caravan floor which had given way. With much determination, therefore, I set aside the week before Mary was due to arrive, telling myself that those few days were to be sacrosanct. Yes, indeed, and whatever happened during them, I was having no visitors to stay.

The week began remarkably quiescent and I made steady progress with the jobs that needed to be done. Alas, it could not last; on the second day the telephone rang in its most demanding fashion. 'Hello,' I said with some caution.

'Hello, Sister Agnes, replied a cheery voice at the other end of the line. 'You don't know me, though we've mutual friends in Fife, which is where I come from. In fact, we're staying in their holiday cottage over on the Shetland Mainland for a few days and they strongly suggested that I ring and ask if we might come over and see you . . . Perhaps stay for a couple of nights and help with any small jobs that you might want doing?'

Firmly and kindly I explained that during this one week in the whole summer I was not going to have anyone to stay. Then, briefly, I explained the reasons why.

'Oh now, that's disappointing,' said the voice, a female voice, with a lovely Scots accent. 'We do understand, of course, though actually, we shall be coming over to Fetlar anyway; we thought for a couple of days.'

'Will you?' I queried. 'And where were you thinking of staying?'

'Oh, at the local guest house. I must ring them right away,' she replied.

'I'm afraid that the guest house isn't functioning at the

moment . . . Oh all right' . . . Look, if you're prepared to be self-catering you can use the big caravan. What did you say your name was?'

'Senga, which will be easy for you to remember, because it's Agnes backwards. And thank you, thank you, Sister Agnes, so much, for allowing us to come. Self-catering, by the way, won't be any problem at all for us.'

I was mowing the lawn when they arrived the next day and was surprised to find that the lady friend whom I had been expecting to arrive with Senga turned out to be her husband, Ned. What a delightful pair they seemed, was my immediate and relieved reaction. I took them indoors and we sat down in the but room and within minutes were talking like old friends. 'The kettle won't be a moment boiling,' I told them, 'so before I take you along to the caravan let's have a cup of tea or coffee or whatever you prefer. I'm sure, after your journey, you'll be needing some refreshment. I certainly do after mowing.'

On the side table in the but room I had the architect's first plans laid out. They had arrived by post that week and I had been perusing his ideas with great excitement. Ned glanced at them in passing and I noticed other more furtive glances in that direction as we sipped our drink. Finally Senga, unable to contain herself longer, whispered in an aside to me, 'You might find it interesting to know that Ned is a quantity surveyor!'

Pulling over the plans with some excitement I told them the sort of things that we were hoping to do.

'They're super plans, though there are various things here that would not pass the Scottish regulations. Let me explain . . .' Ned was a lecturer at Dundee and told me that as a number of his students had been sent to Shetland he was 'in the know' with regard to the building situation up here.

'How super! This is wonderfully providential news, Ned . . . I'm so glad that your wife bullied me into saying you could come!'

Ned chuckled. 'Also,' he went on, 'I could possibly pass you on to one of those old students who is now working permanently in Shetland as a surveyor.'

Despite my initial reluctance to have Senga and Ned to stay, they not only became good friends but were also a tremendous help to me with some of the jobs that I had wanted to get done. Senga did a lot of baking to put in the freezer and Ned, among other things, mended a large area of rotten floor in the caravan.

Soon after they had departed, the great day of Mary's arrival dawned – the 21st July 1989, timed exactly, a year to the day, from her first visit. How elated I was, dotting to and from the back window of the house to see if she were coming. At eleven-thirty her car stopped outside The Ness, crammed with an incalculable array of household bits and pieces from the home that she had shared with her husband, and there, perched on the top, were Aros the cat and Tildy the Australian terrier.

As there had been no need to drive down to the ferry to meet her I had made sure that there was a roaring peat fire in the ben room along with a meal almost ready to serve. Also, I had popped a hot water bottle into her bed in case she was half dead from her two days' journeying from Worcester.

Mary was a marvellous companion, yet I won't say that our first few weeks together were the easiest of our lives; not for either of us. A great deal of adjustment still had to be made on both our parts. For in character we were as different as could be, and saw many aspects of life from contrary viewpoints.

Mary, brought up in a clergy household, had attended boarding school on a scholarship. Laughingly, she had told me that it had not been the happiest of experiences and at the age of thirteen she had been asked to leave, as being ineducable. 'After that, it was the local Secondary Mod for me,' she explained, 'where it was discovered that I needed glasses.' Once her sight had been corrected she had in fact done quite well and gone on to a teacher training college. 'At college,' she informed me, 'I gained a teaching certificate in English, Needlework and Religious Studies plus an extra year's course to gain a certificate in Special Needs.' She went on to say that it was whilst still a young teacher that she met the man who was to become her husband. Meric, a doctor, was a good many years her senior. However, after much serious thought, finally she promised to follow him to Canada where he was about to start a new life. There they married, and since they were not to have children Mary pursued her studies and gained a BA in English and Sociology, a MEd in Guidance and Counselling, and did a further course in the Special Needs field at the University of Toronto.

After eighteen years of marriage her husband suffered a stroke. Eventually, as his condition deteriorated and he was no longer able to work, Mary, through her teaching, continued to keep them afloat. She did this by taking various teaching jobs, which for a period necessitated having to travel a hundred miles to and from school each day. It was at that time that she bought Tildy and Aros as companions for Meric during the long hours he was alone. After a year or so of this unsatisfactory type of existence they made arrangements to return to England. Meric was delighted to be back, though it was not long afterwards that sadly, he died. This happened just two and a half years before she was to join me.

Mary is a vital person, full of ideas and more energy along certain lines than I will ever have. Often, even now, she hides her real, deeper, sensitive self beneath a covering of talk and motion. She is impulsive as well as dynamic, and often disorganised, which in contrast to my own over-tidy, sometimes pernickety, nature has caused many a friction. Also, she is a great believer in spending whatever money seems to be at our disposal. Saving even a five pence piece is abhorrent to her, which can be alarming. Albeit, hand in hand with this side of her nature which some might call Franciscan, she is generous to a degree. In fact, I do not think that I have ever known a greater sharer. Nothing in our home can be counted ours even in trust, if there is someone around with a deeper need.

Another thing which we have had to work at is the bringing together of our spiritual traditions – mine from the Anglo-Catholic side of the Church and hers from the Evangelical. How strange God's ways are, and wonderful, I have often thought: here was Mary, constantly questioning and gnawing away at things regarding liturgy and ceremonial, longing to understand the reason why and to return to basics of scriptural teaching. And here was I, holding firmly to a Christian theology and prescription that I had been taught to depend on and had been nourished by. Both of us, to start with, were reluctant to let go our safeguards, give way or wade into the deep. Mary certainly had been trained to question, especially other people's attitudes, though mostly, or so it seemed to me, having first worked out what her own answers should be. In contrast, my training had been in the art of obediently accepting all that was told me by my spiritual teachers. Therefore, with regard to spiritual matters I armoured myself with that knowledge. It was not surprising then, that when Mary poked what I thought of as irrelevant questions through the chinks of my armour, I bridled. Nor was it surprising that when I threw some of my deepest spiritual concepts at her she refused to listen. She wanted immediate answers, her sort of answers, and I was requesting of her that she accept lock, stock and barrel not only the teaching that I could impart from my heart, but that also which had been rammed into me since I had become a religious.

The only answer of which we were both certain at that time, though we sometimes wondered why, was that God had called her to join me. Often, even now, we remark that the Lord must have a truly marvellous sense of humour!

During my convent years in Devon I had become accustomed to being told what to do and how exactly I was to do it. Rarely, if ever, was I allowed to make any important decisions. Therefore the solitary years on Fetlar were a real time of growth in a mental sense as well as a spiritual one. To start with, I had to re-organise my own life and provide a living for myself. All the same, it was not at all as complicated as living at close quarters and on equal terms with another human being. No wonder that God left me in soak for four and a half years! In a tremendously positive sense Mary and I are good for each other. Certainly she has taught me to reconsider many things that I previously accepted at face value.

We worked through our differences, learning to appreciate each other in the gradual discovery of what made us each tick.

81

Most of all, we learned to love one another for what we really are and consequently to be completely honest. For example, on the occasions when I am buttered up by the general public or the media, or even just a little by the community, then my dear friend, who has a deep loathing for plaster saints, goes into action in her capacity of being my PPP, a title role she long ago bestowed on herself, which in full reads: Personal Pedestal Polisher.

A week or so after Mary joined me, Frances came up to Fetlar, as planned, for part of the school summer holidays. At the same time another friend, Viv, who is a middle-aged widow with a grown-up family, descended upon us for three weeks. Viv had been a school mistress and had adored teaching teenagers. However, at some point during the previous year she had suddenly, after a lightning call, changed direction, the outcome being that she was accepted for training in the ministry course at Salisbury Theological College. After this she had read my first book, put herself in touch, and we had struck up a correspondence. Finally this led to her asking to come and stay for a week, before her first term began at Salisbury.

That first visit of Viv's was a happy one in which our friendship was cemented and in which, also, she fell deeply in love with Shetland. Looking back now to her holiday, two things especially stand out in my mind. The first was that she greatly encouraged me to go ahead with the possible building project idea. Secondly, and this was a bolt from the blue, she admitted before she left that if she had not promised to go to Salisbury she would have asked to join me! I can still hear my astonished reply: 'Vivien, since Salisbury came first then I think that we must assume that that is where you're meant to go, certainly to start with.' She dutifully and wisely agreed and later, during her time at college, kept closely in touch. A year later she asked to return for a second stay.

So it was that Viv returned to Fetlar soon after Mary arrived to test her vocation. Mary was received as SOLI's first postulant. Having Frances meant that we could learn some new music for the occasion and so, after a series of very jolly choir practices, Father Lewis arrived to take a memorable and lovely service in the byre/chapel. The date was August 1989.

The holiday passed quickly and in no time at all it was time for Frances and Viv to return south. We had had many talks during their stay, especially about the future. Viv was now toying with the idea of perhaps one day being able to work at some kind of ministry in Shetland. 'It might not happen for some years, especially since I've now been asked to do the degree course. Also, however I qualify, a job such as I'm trained for is going to be hard to come by in Shetland . . . Ah well,' she sighed philosophically, 'it's all in the Lord's hands. If He wants me here He will help make it possible.'

Frances was able to be more definite and asked if she could come and settle with us as soon as she retired from teaching the following summer. 'Would it be possible to come in the same capacity as Rosemary, as an associate member? There's nothing that I would like better than to spend my retirement in being attached to such a group as yourselves. Of course, I could only help in small, rather insignificant ways and you'd often have to tell me what to do and how exactly to do it. Some things could be useful, though, at least I think they could – such as helping in the garden, giving visitors a cup of tea, doing a little shopping, collecting folk from the ferry, and so on.'

'Frances, dear Frances, we'd love to have you join us and I, too, can't think of anything nicer. Really, you're being inordinately modest, for you've a great deal to offer us. A true commitment to start with, and then such qualities as gentleness of spirit, the willingness to do anything you're asked, however trivial, joyfulness in doing it and not least, your expertise in the music field. How splendid it's going to be to have a resident organist for all those special occasions, and you know without me telling you how absolutely shocking our plainsong is. You've got your work cut out there before you come.'

'Oh thank you, thank you . . . I'm really thrilled. It'll be a year, of course, before I can come and there'll be some sort of accommodation to be sorted out too.'

'With regard to long-term accommodation I'd greatly like you to take on The Ness, to become a sort of gate-keeper, if that recommends itself to you, though that's of course with the proviso that Sandy, my landlord, will approve . . . and if you'd like to?'

There was a muted burble from Frances, and then: 'Sister Agnes, I'm speechless . . . I can't think of anything lovelier.'

'Yes, well, I'd a feeling that you might be asking to join us, or, if I'm being honest, I should say that I was hoping you would and had therefore given some thought to all these possibilities. You won't be able to move in of course until we have built SOLI's Home Centre out on the headland. So accommodation will need to be found temporarily for you, especially since Mary and I and all the little animals and visitors are cramped enough as it is in The Ness. As for the time factor, we think it best that anyone wishing to come has at least a year to prepare. We say that for every reason, not simply because the lifestyle here is rigorous.

'Oh yes, I do understand that and can't thank you enough. My cup's just brimming over. It'll be wonderful to be of some assistance in a simple way. Don't forget, you'll have to tell me what to do, though!'

Mary's commitment was to be a complete one and presented even fewer difficulties than Frances'. It was Rose's call that still puzzled me.

Yes, I had received a strong confirmative note from Rose whilst she had been on Iona. Whilst there, away from her demanding life, she had had time and space to think and really consider her future. Then, wham, bang! inspiration and the answer had come to her and she had written this unexpected and treasured letter from that holy isle. Suddenly, it seems, it had become crystal clear that she should come to Fetlar despite any element of risk, though in exactly what capacity was still not certain.

Neither could I see at all clearly where Rose would fit happily into the community. That is, until one afternoon whilst I was writing in the neuk and the answer, out of almost nothingness, slotted itself into my mind. At that moment I was certainly not thinking about anything but my letters. However, both Rose and Viv had been much in my prayers so perhaps it was not so surprising that the answer was suddenly laid before me, and why ever had I not thought of it before? Yes, it was obvious and so possible – they must both have a dual vocation. I could be wrong, of course, though why not? Why not have such people, who could participate in the life at the centre here on Fetlar and at the same time reach out further afield, using their own training and gifts? In a sense they would be radiating out and drawing in as well as keeping us at the centre in touch with what was happening on the shop floor. In that moment a new and wider concept of what SOLI was meant to be or what it could be, framed itself in the form of a diagram in my mind. The most exciting bit, it seemed to me, was the fact that organically it could be divided if it became too large and secondly, there was nothing hierarchical about its government.

1. *God the centre and hub of our life*

2. *The Sisters in vows*

The inner circle is very small, yet a strength to the wheel. It covers no ground like the outer circle, though helps it to go round and forward. It takes the weight of the wheel, all the spokes lead to it and from it. It is a place of prayer, a place providing strength and refreshment; it is a concentrated area which holds the spokes tightly together, drawing them into the hub. These Sisters, called the Ark, and belonging to this home centre of SOLI, would be home-centred – that is, not dispersed into professional jobs or any form of work away from home, their role being:

> to live the gospel in simplicity and joy;
> to recite the Divine Offices;
> to be available to the needs of others;
> to provide hospitality to visitors;
> to support through prayer and correspondence.

3. *Oblate Sisters* (spokes)

The Oblate Sisters are the active part of SOLI, in the sense that they radiate out and draw in. They work with and touch those on the shop floor through their dual vocation to SOLI and to their nursing, teaching, serving or ministering in some other way. They share the life of the community when at home and at other times reach out to wider areas.

4. *Associates*
The middle circle takes some of the strain and weight from the centre and is made up of a group of friends who have chosen to live around us and who participate in our daily life. They share our work, give hospitality and are available, acting as a strengthening and supporting element, protecting the Sisters from too many distractions.

5. *The Caim*
The outer circle is made up of a large group of friends, men and women, who wish to be close supporters though they live their own lives away from the community. They are known as the Caim – *caim* is a Celtic word meaning 'encompassment' or 'the circle around'. These people support us in prayer, offer practical and/or financial help according to their means, follow a simple lifestyle and are available to others in need within their own communities.

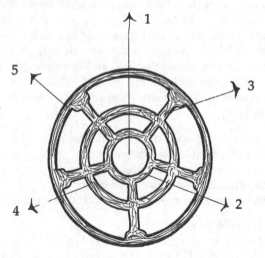

> Come, O Creator Spirit, come,
> And make within our hearts thy home;
> To us thy grace celestial give
> Who of thy breathing move and live.[1]

It's Whit Sunday again, and as the plainsong of our Office hymn soars upwards to disappear into the rafters of the byre/chapel and out through the chinks in the walls and doors, a wondrous concept in my mind is caught up in a single thought. A thought that is the answer to an intricate maze of questions which have been buzzing around my mind and for which I've long been seeking an answer.

How complex we make our lives, in that we search and scratch our heads, struggle to write our answers across a blank sheet of paper and try so hard to find the meaning of a question, a problem or an issue that we constantly bypass because it's far too simple.

Soon I need to work out and make a written statement regarding the community's Rule of Life, with the community's approval. Every religious order is under an obligation to do this and to present it to the authorities within the Church. The authorities are entitled to an official declaration regarding the way of life and all aspects of it – about the three vows of Poverty, Chastity and Obedience, about the spirit of the community and about such things as its work, prayer, novitiate, silences, free time, the religious habit, holidays, etc.

My spirit has been working overtime on the intricacies of all this, and the results, to my mind, are totally unsatisfactory. Yet suddenly, I know in a thought and beyond all doubt what the answer is, and it's the answer for every chapter of SOLI's rule and SOLI's life. For what is our poverty but the Poverty of Love, and our obedience but the Obedience of Love, and our chastity but the Chastity of Love? Yes, what a different concept it becomes when they are not just things for their own sake but for the sake of Him who is Love.

> As in the past
> It is now
> It will last
> It will grow
> It will be
> To eternity

87

The Love of God.
May it be so
In ebb and flow,
May it remain
In wax and wane,
The Love of God
It shall be
To eternity.

Father attend
Jesus befriend
Spirit defend
By sea
By shore
Evermore
By land
By sea
Let it be
Evermore
Let it be
Eternally.[2]

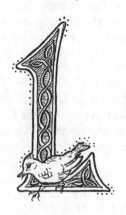

L for LARK

9 Feather Frail

As summer moved into autumn, the oyster catchers, whimbrels and other migratory birds flew south to warmer climes. The colour of the grass turned to a burnished gold and a sneaky wind infiltrated the house around the outer door of The Ness.

In the middle of November, Sybil, a retired nurse from Reading, arrived for her winter break on Fetlar. She had learned about us two years previously through her friend Jill, who one morning had slipped a copy of *A Tide that Sings* through her letter-box. Sybil, who had been hoovering, heard a thud, switched off the hoover and scurried to the door. There on the door mat was this interesting-looking package. Picking it up she had unwrapped it and sat on the sofa to investigate further. Discovering that it was a paperback, the personal story of a nun's life in Shetland, she flicked through the pages to look at the drawings and then glanced at the opening paragraphs. Several hours later, with only a chapter to go, and with a strangely warm and excited glow inside, she had, she told me months afterwards, unrepentantly put away the vacuum cleaner.

Soon after this episode she wrote telling us a little about herself, how she had nursed her sister through cancer and then repeated the same caring service for a close friend. 'Now,' she said, 'I am alone with no real family at all, though I must tell you that Jill and I both belong to a small, helpful Julian Group that, incidentally, would like to become Prayer Partners with SOLI.' We were soon linked with her group in this way and remember each other on Thursdays. Sybil continued to write and later informed me that she had arranged a short holiday to Fetlar.

As she was too shy to ask to come and stay with me, she made alternative arrangements to 'bide' with my dear friends Mimie, Kenny and Anne, who gave hospitality to visitors. On the Sunday that she was on the isle I collected Mimie as usual, to drive to the kirk; it was then that Sybil and I met. A fragile white-haired lady stood waiting at the gate with Mimie. Later, I was to learn that this seemingly elderly lady, full of boundless energy, was a great walker and would not have thought twice about walking the three miles or so to the kirk. Opening the back door of the old banger I asked them, respectfully, to get in as fast as they could. Coughing and spluttering, the car engine, I knew, would stall and perhaps refuse to function at all unless we moved away quickly. 'Sorry about the front passenger seat too, Mimie,' I yelled above the cacophony of noise. 'Its back's given way as you can see.' Sybil, smiling wanly, passed the time of day, and apart from driving them home after the service, that was the first and last that we saw of each other until the day before she left.

So many people write and are in touch, that unfortunately I had not associated this retiring little lady as the person who had written such strong letters to me from Reading. So it was not until her last day when she plucked up courage to visit The Ness that I discovered my *faux pas*. Filled with shame, I showed her around and gave her tea. She was extremely forgiving and in no time at all we had become good friends and had a jolly time.

'Sybil, why on earth didn't you tell me who you were, sooner? Now look what we've done . . . you're having to shoot off home when we've just got to know each other. I'd have so liked you to have met Rosemary, too.'

'Sorry,' she said, then leaning towards me in a conspiratorial manner, whispered, 'I'm hoping to come back in a few months' time. It's perhaps naughty – but I don't think I can stay away!'

So that was how Sybil began to visit Fetlar twice a year, and how during this cold blustery November she came with the special reason of being received as a Caim member. We held a simple little service tucked away into the tiny oratory chapel, and afterwards a celebratory supper. Dear Sybil, she was moved to tears and could hardly tell us how special and how much the occasion meant to her. 'Sister Agnes,' she breathed at a point when we were both alone, 'it's as though I've been confirmed all over again.'

Sybil's time went as quickly as ever and on the last evening as she was getting into the car to be driven back to Mimie's house she asked if we would say a special prayer for her. 'Could you ask God to help me to make a right decision about a problem which I'm not going to explain to you about this minute but which is of great importance to me? Please?' she begged.

'Of course we will, Sybil, and we'll pray that He'll give you the right answer soon. Though don't forget that "*all* things," whatever they are, do "work together for good" if we really love God. I'm sure of this, despite the fact that it might not be in quite the way we'd hoped.'

After Sybil's return to Reading the Christmas mail began to pile in and in the midst of it, and all of a flurry, we began our preparations for Mary's great day. Father Lewis and I had talked together of the occasion and then consulted with our good friend and boss, Bishop Frederick. We all decided that since Mary was to be a founder member of the community and would need to take on a certain amount of the responsibility, she should not only be clothed in the religious habit but at the same time be allowed to make her first vows.

Mary and I worked hard on the making of our new habits. For these, we had bought a roll of oatmeal-coloured Shetland tweed and now cut, measured and machined it into simple full-length tunics. They looked comfortable, warm and not un-attractive, especially when we had the knotted Franciscan cords tied around our waists, and scapulars on top.

The date decided upon for the service was 8th December, the great festival of Our Lady Immaculate, which incidentally, was the same date as the fifth anniversary of my leaving the convent in Devon. Hundreds of people write to me over Christmas, and Advent becomes less and less the gentle season that I used to love. Therefore, with various other jobs piling up amongst the 'Christmas is coming' clamour, we were severely pressed to meet this deadline.

Winds raged around the house the night before Mary's Pro-fession and we stayed up into the early hours finishing off the habits, preparing for the service and doing some extra baking, for we had invited about thirty people to come and share the day with us. Among these were Mimie, Kenny and Anne, Alma and Dennis, Magnus the minister, and the Dean of Aberdeen and Orkney whom we had asked to preach.

The morning dawned cold and windless, with blue skies. Mary, in semi-retreat until 11.45 a.m. when the service was to begin, took my advice and did a vanishing act. She told me later that she had walked to Haliara-kirk!

We had been able to afford just one or two pot plants for decoration and had only resorted to buying them because any outdoor flowers in this climate have long since disappeared by December; indeed, the gardens are quite bare even of foliage by then. However, with what we had bought placed in just the right position, the effect was delightful and the byre/chapel that day was beautiful in its simplicity. What I had kept as an enormous surprise, though, was a huge bouquet of dazzling blooms sent to Mary from all our friends at Holy Cross Church, Edingburgh. Those, I decided, should be saved for a grand presentation at the end of the service.

John, a young man and our nearest neighbour, was the first to arrive. He was cumbered about, almost from head to foot, with all kinds of professional-looking contraptions for recording the service on video. Before going into the chapel he filmed the views around The Ness, the sun streaming over the sea, the warm colours of the stone buildings and the lights and shades of the hills and fields. Then, in he swung through the open door of the waiting chapel, still partly a byre. Its rough woodwork formed simple pews around the lectern and the altar and upon the latter, on the left-hand side, the new habit for Mary was neatly folded. Along with the habit was placed a silver ring, designed with Celtic interlacings, which she was to wear as a symbol of her unending love and faithfulness to God. Through the skylight windows shafts of sunlight flooded the quiet scene with pools of light. 'Clare, clarity, light . . . a good name for her,' I mused.

Sadly, Rose and Frances were unable to get away from their jobs in the south to be with us for the occassion and without them, we noted, our family felt incomplete. What a joy it would have been, too, to have had Frances at the organ providing us with the music and in her insistent way making sure that we sang the right notes. Actually, an electronic organ had been very kindly donated to us by a member of the Caim, and we were longing to use it. However, Eunice, the wife of our Presbyterian minister, bravely stepping in to take Frances' place, brought her own organ which she insisted she was more familiar with. Seating herself she began to play. Friends filtered in, Rosemary saw them to their places and I made my way back to the house to see if Mary was ready. She was dressing when I arrived and in the process of pulling a clean navy-blue sweater over her head.

'How are you doing? Have you got everything you need?' I asked.

'Yes, I think so. Oh, Sister, could you possibly get me a clean hankie, please?'

When I returned she was completely clad in her postulant's garb: navy-blue skirt, fisherman's smock, jumper and a small scarf tied around her head. She smiled nervously and I hugged her to me.

'Don't want to change your mind?' I queried.

'No, definitely not . . . now, or ever,' she replied.

'Let's go then.'

As we entered the crowded chapel and were moving towards our seats at the front of it, I noticed, to my consternation, that the candles had not been lit; seeing also the heads of the clergy beginning to appear around one of the cattle stalls at the back of the byre, I snatched up a taper and a box of matches. Quickly, yet as gracefully as I could, for there were at least two dozen candles to light, I hoped that I was giving the impression that this was the way we normally did things. The clergy made their way to the altar as I wove in and out of various obstacles, stretching my taper back and forth. The organ changed its theme, I sank into my seat and glanced across at Mary, knowing that a new chapter had begun.

All that we had in the chapel for warmth were two small gas heaters strategically placed in the vicinity of the older people. However, despite the piercing coldness it was a wonderful service – though how we all laughed when later at Kenny and Mimie's home, we saw the video. For there we all were with what looked like enormous balloons of smoke billowing from our mouths and singing, 'Breathe on me, Breath of God'! Yes, the 'smoke', of course, was the breath from our own mouths hitting the cold air.

John made a supremely professional job of the filming and has thus given us the privilege and pleasure, on rare, special occasions, of reliving the ceremony.

With Mary kneeling before the rough wooden altar, the service progressed as she made her Declaration of Intent:

> 'I wish to be clothed in the habit of the Society of Our Lady of the Isles. I seek to give myself to the Lord Jesus; to live according to the gospel in the manner inspired by St Francis and St Clare – living a simple life of prayer, study and work; to allow the Holy Spirit to bring forth his fruit in my life and in particular the virtues of humility, love and joy.'

Next, Father Lewis blessed the habit and then laid it in her arms saying:

> 'Put on the full armour of God. Stand firm with the belt of truth buckled round your waist, the breastplate of righteousness in place and with your feet fitted with the readiness that comes from the gospel of peace. Take also the shield of faith, with which you can extinguish all the flaming arrows of the evil one. Accept salvation as a helmet and the word of God as the sword which the spirit gives you. Do all this in prayer, asking for God's help.'[1]

Mary stood and the strains of the organ again filled the air. This time the music was the introduction to the next hymn, the longest, most suitable one that we could find: 'Just as I am, without one plea'. As the congregation launched forth into the first verse she and I wended our way to the tiny room at the back of the chapel which was temporarily being used as a sacristy. Shutting the door firmly behind us we then, as quickly as we could, pushed and pulled her into her new garb.

'You look lovely,' I told her, pulling the cord a little more tightly around her waist, 'and I think that they're just starting on the last verse. We've done well. Ready to reappear then?'

'Yes,' she whispered. 'Do I really look all right?'

Standing back at arms' length I looked her critically up and down. Oh, just a minute, you've a lock of hair sticking out of your headband on this side. Let me tuck it in for you . . . Good, that's better.'

As we re-entered the chapel almost everyone seemed to be peering in our direction over the top of their service sheets. Father Lewis, too, was glancing around and, thinking that we might need a few more minutes, was just suggesting that the first verses should be sung again. He smiled delightedly when he saw us and beckoned to Eunice to fade out the music.

From this point the service continued with Mary being given her new name and being invited to make her vows of poverty, chastity and obedience for a period of no less than one year. She knelt again and, with me standing beside her, made her pledge:

> 'In the Name of the most holy and undivided
> Trinity and in honour of the glorious Virgin
> Mary Mother of God. I, Sister Mary Clare,
> dedicate my life to God. I promise to live in
> Chastity, Obedience and Poverty for one year
> and according to the rule of the Society of Our
> Lady of the Isles. I give myself wholly to
> God's Divine Love, to spend and be spent in
> his Holy Service.'

The vows, which were temporary, that is, to be renewed for up to five consecutive years before making them for life, were received by Father Lewis. After which, he blessed the silver ring and placed it on her finger, before finally handing her a lighted candle as the sign of the Light of Christ.

As the service drew to a close I looked for an opportune moment to sneak away and retrieve the surprise bouquet to present to her after the last hymn. However, as I was about to move out of my place I, myself, was landed with a bolt from the blue.

Father Lewis slightly raised a hand in my direction to stay my exit and then turned around to face the congregation. 'This part of the service has not been allowed for on the service sheets and is, I'm unashamed to say, going to come as something of a surprise to both Sister Agnes and Rosemary. Will you all please sit.'

'Firstly,' he said, 'since the candle that Sister Agnes received at her Life Profession service in 1969 was left behind in the convent in Devon, we thought it fitting to give her another identical with the one given a little while ago to our new Sister, Mary Clare. This, also, can be as a symbol of the Light of Christ to Sister Agnes and as a reminder of her dedication with Sister Mary Clare, to God, in their religious life together, beginning anew today in this place.'

The candle had a beautiful piece of white ribbon tied around it, as had Sister Mary Clare's, and as Father handed it to me with a kiss I felt quite overcome. Then, as if that was not enough, I was given a Celtic-designed ring myself, not a silver band as was Sister Mary Clare's but a gold ring shaped in the form of the St Ninian Cross, which was found up here in Shetland on St Ninian's Isle. This was given me as Foundress of the new community, and to the joy of all of us, Rosemary too was given an identical ring in silver as a thank you to her for all her loyalty and love in supporting me and as a mark of her leadership of the Caim.

As the last hymn was sung, I collected the bouquet of flowers from its hiding place and presented it to my first Sister in vows. How staggered and overjoyed she was, for there are few things she likes more than flowers. Afterwards, photographs were taken and then in a convoy of cars we rode to the island hall. In the hall the young women of the isle, led by our friend Anne, had prepared us a meal. Sister Mary Clare, as a bit of an anti-climax, christened her new habit by spilling soup on its skirt, though I must add in her defence that it was really my fault. That, however, is another story which I am not telling.

This lovely season when we meditate on the coming of Jesus is once again almost over, and as I sit and wait for the community to join me for the First Vespers of the Fourth Sunday in Advent I am especially conscious of the simplicity and love that accompanied the arrival of God's Son.

My thoughts are thrusting around in the few minutes that I have, seeking out new glimmers, new facets of the truth. And yes, in that poor stable, a stable such as the one in which I sit, I understand afresh that Jesus arrived as we arrived into the world, naked, helpless and vulnerable. He was in need of a love which would clothe and nourish him, and his parents, as ours, responded to that need. Like us, he was dependent upon love, a special kind of love which is not just a necessity during our infant years but abides with us for ever; of this I feel sure. In this concept of it, it seems to me that we can look to being fed and clothed into eternity, for I believe that we cannot live either now or in that heaven to come without love.

I've had to pull my cloak around me to keep out the draughts. Now, warmer, I thank God for all that he's given us . . . Yes, Love is the provider of all things and without it we are spiritually dead. So then, is that love which is so freely given to us by God, also a sacrament? And as a sacrament does it have an inward and an outward sign? Do what we wear and what we eat, outwardly show in measure who it is, who in love nourishes us?

Skerry, who's just jumped on to my lap, is twisting around and around making ready to flop into a comfortable position. Ah, he's done it, and is purring loudly. 'Skerry, you're a lovely hot water bottle,' I tell him and close my eyes.

One of the pieces of Scripture which drew me as a teenager towards giving my whole life to God was: 'Take no thought for your life, what ye shall eat; neither for the body, what ye shall out on.'[2] Having taken this to heart I've found that a life given to God is nourished and cared for and that one does not have to be anxious about its inner needs, for all those are taken care of. Yes, that must be it, that sustained from within we are able to radiate an inner strength, warmth and well-being through our outer, earthly garb. It was said of St Francis that his earthly life had worn so thin that the heavenly shone through him.

I think that as children of a Father who is Love we need not spend time worrying about our warmth and nourishment. For, although some find it hard to believe, our inner needs are and will be catered for. We can turn from God's care, of course, for we have the freedom of choice. Yet also, we can accept it and grow.

What then of our outer garb, the religious habit, I ask? I am aware of Sister Mary Clare's challenging remarks about this, to which I have stuffed my ears for months.

Firstly, for me, the habit has always been the outward sign of a life totally and inwardly given to God, though the danger here is (and who says that life is without dangers?) that the life that has been given, can in some cases be retrieved by the giver and then hidden behind the habbit. Also, and perhaps worse, the habit itself can hide God.

Despite these appalling possibilities I do feel in my heart that a habit is a good thing. For a common garb helps to bind a community on equal terms and squashes those hierarchical tendencies that lead so rampantly in the direction of rank and superiority. Also, the habit means that the whole of the community outwardly look the same, at least at a first glance. Take a second one though, I smile to myself, and you will find that in some religious and indeed in secular folk too, that the outer clothing has worn so thin that the inner garment of God's love shines out.

Some religious communities have become completely secular in their religious dress. They say that to wear ordinary clothes brings one closer to ordinary people. Yet I wonder . . . Perhaps to wear ordinary clothes makes us less like religious? The danger again, to my mind, is that with secular clothing it often leads to fashion-consciousness, rivalry and often expense, especially amongst a group of women. When a nun relinquishes her veil she then needs to think about how her hair looks. When she stops wearing a long habit, which incidentally is just the right type of garment to wear in our Shetland climate, she has to start buying nylon tights or some other equivalent, and so it goes on.

Skerry is poking his head out of his cloak nest on my lap, for there is the sound of footsteps. 'It's all right,' I whisper, and he's ducked down again into the warmth, quickly realising that it's only Rosemary and Frances.

So then, bearing all the pros and cons in mind, what do we do about this habit question?

Rosemary switches on the lights as she comes in and Frances, following her, has struck a match, lit a taper and is lighting the altar candles. Trying not to disturb Skerry any sooner than necessary, I bend forward carefully and pick up my Office Book.

Well, I decide, still pursuing my stream of thought, my conclusion can only be that we bear the exhortation of Jesus in our hearts. That is, that leaning upon the love of God we have no anxious thoughts in our minds. Perhaps we should do this, in the sense that we don't make mountains out of molehills or make enormous issues out of such questions. Let us be moderate, letting our 'moderation be known unto all men' and let us walk between our options with an open mind.

For ourselves here on Fetlar, we will continue to dress as simply as we can in what is provided, which for us, is a blue scarf, a Shetland spun, natural-coloured full-length tunic on Sundays and Holy Days and a fisherman's smock and 'breeks' during the week. Yet whatever we wear, may the love and joy of God shine from our hearts and radiate through our garb. For again our Lord says that 'Life is more than meat, and the body is more than raiment. Consider the ravens: for they neither sow nor reap; which neither have storehouses nor barn; and God feedeth them: how much more are ye better than the fowls?'[3]

I am conscious suddenly of Sister Mary Clare sitting beside me and that the Office has begun. Verse and verse about of the psalms are alternately being recited from this side and that of the chapel. From Rosemary and Frances, then from us two Sisters, back and forth in ebb and flow like the pulse beat of the heart the psalms are said. Until, on our feet, Sister Mary Clare who is the precentor for this week, is reading in a clear and audible voice the Little Chapter for this Office of the Fourth Sunday in Advent:

> Brethren, rejoice in the Lord alway:
> and again I say, rejoice. Let your
> moderation be known unto all men.
> The Lord is at hand.[4]

10 Wafted Westwards

After our guests had returned home we settled down once again for the winter. Christmas came and went with all its solemnity and fun and as usual it was for me a very busy time indeed, answering the heavy mail that came in. Excitingly, large unexpected donations arrived too and the Building Fund went up to four thousand pounds. We could hardly believe it, though we knew that that would not even cover the levelling of the site. However, it was a wonderful start in so short a time and we were full of hope.

Unusually, the winter was a mild one and before we knew where we were it had merged into the spring. At least, we were given that impression. Lulled into quietude we were little prepared for a month of fierce gales in March. Rose had written to say that she would arrive in March, and that she had bought a small caravan to use as temporary accommodation. It was a good sturdy one and we thought that perhaps later we might use it as a hermitage. We called it Greenbank, partly after the house on Iona where Rosemary and I had first stayed and where I had heard my call to come north; partly because its own tradename, stamped on the front of its bodywork, was Greenbank; and partly because we sited it in the shelter of a large green mound.

Greenbank arrived a little before Rose did, during a week slashing with rain, and we had a very muddy time getting the site finally prepared and manoeuvring the caravan into position. However, the rain cleared up the week before she arrived and we built some fencing around part of the caravan to act as an added protection against the wind. Rose was thrilled with her sea view and the streamers and the 'Welcome' notice dangling across Greenbank's large front window. It was a darling place to be and she loved it – except during the nights when the tail end of the winter lashed around. Despite all our efforts to protect the caravan from the elements, despite the ropes that Sister Mary Clare and I had one night in panic thrown over the top and anchored it down with, it still 'bucked like a bronco', Rose told us. In fact, one night she had been so alarmed that she tottered out of bed, dressed, and with her pillows tucked under her arm had stepped outside in the hopes of being able to reach The Ness, a hundred feet or so away. Half expecting to be blasted out over the North Sea to the Outer Skerries she clung tightly to the fence as she struggled to shut the door. Extraordinarily, she found that it seemed less wild outside than it had within. 'They will think that I'm foolish,' she thought. 'I'd better go back in and ride it out.' So she returned to her tempest-tossed bed and listened to the banshee wailing of the wind.

The Building Fund, which had started so encouragingly, became stuck in a deep rut and did not move at all during that tempestuous spring. At about this time we heard that some croft houses on the island of Yell were up for sale, the prices ranging from between two and four thousand pounds. Sister Mary Clare became very excited about this and due to our growing numbers, suggested that we abandon our building plans and consider buying one with the money we had. I was what is rudely known these days as gobstopped! 'Oh, I know that Yell is about six miles over the water,' she went on, 'yet soon we're desperately going to need space and if we actually owned property then there would be a chance that we could enlarge.'

'No, no, no!' I exploded. 'I may have been reluctant to build to start with, but it's now abundantly clear, beyond all doubt, certainly to me, that this is the direction that God's asking us to travel.'

'What about Frances when she comes in August? Where are we going to put her?'

'She won't mind having the big caravan temporarily,' I retorted, though I did not feel a hundred per cent sure in myself that it was really a good plan, especially after Rose's experience. However, what I *was* certain of at that moment was that we should not change course at this stage, and as far as I was concerned the discussion was closed.

By the afternoon post that day came a letter from a lady in

Stirling which was, in part, to solve a little of our accommodation problem. We read the letter with growing excitement. It told us that she had a little cottage on the Shetland Mainland which she would like some group to use for a Christian purpose, and were we interested.

'How wonderful,' we shrieked. 'And at this particular moment!'

'Well, let's go over to the Shetland Mainland and see it as soon as we can, Sister Mary Clare,' I smiled.

'Quite, quite amazing,' she answered.

The owner of the house, Chris, with her husband Peter and their two children, lived in Stirling and they were later to become good friends of ours. That afternoon I rang her for the first time, saying how interested we were in the possibility of renting the property even though it was about sixty miles and two ferries from Fetlar. She told me where I could obtain the key and I made arrangements with her to go over and have a look at the house later in the same week. So, on a grey overcast spring day we travelled over to Da Gaets for the first time.

The stone cottage sat at the end of a long, sparsely-populated valley; a beautiful, hilly, isolated spot. The single-track road that wound its way to it, possibly meandering along the course of an old sheep track, came to an abrupt end almost on a level with the guttering on the back of the building. Larger than The Ness, it lay snuggled into the folds of a high moorland slope, its front windows looking out on to the rocky contours of the hill opposite. Beyond its tiered garden shimmered an expanse of water. This water ran down from the hills and out into the sea. During the winter months the loch is high and sparkling whereas in the summer it is just a marshy bog, though full of wild iris and rare birds. A footpath runs from the garden, which incidentally was full of overgrown shrubs and plants rarely seen in Shetland. Da Gaets, situated in this most beautiful spot, lived up to its name, which is a Shetland word meaning 'the way' or, 'the footpath', and indeed had its own little footpath down to the sea about five minutes' walk away.

The inside of the house was not as attractive but damp and mousey and dark too, for the last tenant had favoured black paint. We felt that it had great potential and asked Chris what she considered a suitable rent might be. She suggested something like ten pounds per week, if we could manage that amount. We knew that as houses go, even here in Shetland, it was amazingly cheap, though we realised that for us, even with the five of us, it would be a great struggle. Deciding that it would be worth it, however, we said yes. Almost immediately Nona, a friend of Rosemary's who was staying with her about that time and who was full of encouragement about the venture, gave us a gift of two hundred pounds. This unexpected donation paid the rent for a good long period of time – long enough for us to fall in love with the place, which we use as a hermitage. Da Gaets also has its uses as a lovely place which we can offer to our visitors from the south who want to see something of the Shetland Mainland. However, because of its remoteness, we tell anyone wishing to stay there that they must have some form of transport. For us it proved useful too, especially when Rose worked for a long period at the hospital in Lerwick. During the week she stayed at Da Gaets and drove home to Fetlar for her days off. Sister Mary Clare and I use it if we have visitors to meet or see off, or if we have shopping or business to do in Lerwick and cannot return easily in one day.

During our first stay at Da Gaets a rather interesting and providential thing happened. Having settled in with the intention of enjoying a happy few days' decorating, suddenly in the midst of slapping lighter-coloured paint over the walls and woodwork, the telephone rang. We almost jumped out of our skins for we have always tried to keep the telephone number of this house private, as primarily it is for us a place of retreat. Only because the house is in such an isolated spot do we keep the telephone there at all. Wiping my hands quickly I picked up the receiver and found to my surprise that the voice at the other end of the line was that of a Yorkshire man.

'Is that Sister Agnes?' he asked.

'Yes it is,' I returned, wondering how on earth the word had got around so quickly that we were there.

'You'll be wondering why I'm ringing,' he went on, 'but I'm a neighbour of yours and live over the hill in the next valley. I used to cut peats for the last tenant who lived at Da Gaets and I was wondering . . . well, I wondered if you'd mind me coming round to pay you a visit . . . this morning?'

I looked down at my disreputable self. 'If you don't mind taking us as you find us, come round and have coffee.'

'Thank you, I'm on my way.'

'Sister Mary Clare,' I yelled towards the kitchen, 'put the kettle on, we've a visitor coming.'

'Oh no, I don't believe it. How long have we got?'

'He said that he would be round right away,' I chortled, stuffing this and that here and there. 'About fifteen minutes I should think.'

As the clock ticked around we waited and waited, feeling somewhat stymied at not being able to get on with the jobs in hand.

'Oh, I give up,' said Sister Mary Clare eventually. 'Shall I start the lunch?'

'Mmm, do. I'll take Tildy up the road as she hasn't had her run this morning.'

A moment or two later there was a loud rap on the door. With Tildy wiggling at my feet encouraging me to go out, I stretched a hand towards the knob and swung open the door. 'Do come in.' I beckoned to our new Yorkshire friend and at the same time pulled off my jacket, much to Tildy's displeasure.

Richard was a large, craggy kind of man, with an easy manner, much younger than I had imagined from our telephone conversation. A little surprised that he did not apologise for being two hours late, we discovered during our chat over coffee that he had walked to us, which had meant an arduous climb over the high ridge between his home and ours.

Sister Mary Clare brought in a snack and as we ate it with him he told us a little about himself and how over the previous year he had built a tiny house for the amazing price of ten thousand pounds.

'How much? Could you say that again?' we cried, gaping in astonishment. 'You see,' we proffered, 'we're terribly interested in such things ourselves at the moment.'

His eyes sparkled as animatedly he went on to tell us how, with a builder friend, he had looked around for cheap, often secondhand materials and then built most of the structure himself. 'For example, I got all the roofing tiles for a tenner.'

'Wow,' said Sister Mary Clare, unusually speechless.

We offered to take him home at the end of our happy get-together, partly so that we might see his fascinating house and partly so that he could show us where the Da Gaets peat banks were. They lay about a mile along the single-track valley road and, we could see, would be easy enough to get to with a vehicle of some kind. As for his house, it was beautifully simple in a Scandinavian type of way and gave us a whole new concept of what we ourselves might do. We realised afresh that we must simplify our ideas even more than we already had, that we could as an alternative option build in wood, and possibly in small units. Perhaps unit by unit as we could afford it.

'There's a building contractor out at Bixter who builds

wooden chalet units,' said Sister Mary Clare as we were driving back to Da Gaets. 'They built those darling little houses that we pass on the Twatt Clousta road. You know, those tiny squarish-looking ones that we've been so intrigued with each time we pass. What about arranging to go and see someone there to talk about what's possible?'

So the next day we went to see Mr Tulloch of Tulloch Construction. He thought that our new plans were good and perfectly feasible, though added that very soon he would be folding up the construction side of his business with the idea of retiring abroad. 'I'm wanting to live somewhere that's a little warmer,' he smiled, 'and am not looking for further work.'

Often, I have found that when working on a project, one can get horribly derailed, and whilst in this state, it seems to me that God puts everything on to hold . . . Once back on the rails again, then whoosh! in a remarkable way, off one goes. For us, in this instance, as soon as we clambered back by simplifying our ideas, the Building Fund was given an enormous boost. Arriving home after those few days at Da Gaets, we found an exciting-looking letter awaiting us from a firm of solicitors in Aberdeen, advising me that a client of theirs, who wished to remain anonymous, wanted to give us a gift of money for the Building Fund. 'Could you tell us,' they asked, 'to whom we make out the cheque?' I lost no time in writing back and about a week later the cheque arrived. Sister Mary Clare and I had returned to Da Gaets for a couple of days to finish off our jobs, and knowing that the money could arrive had asked Rosemary to open that particular envelope and give us a ring to tell us how much had been donated.

'It's come,' said Rosemary down the telephone in a remarkably calm voice. 'Guess how much?'

'Will it be a lovely surprise?' I wheedled.

'A really super one, but you must guess.'

'Right, well, we think between three and five hundred pounds. Are we near?'

'No, wrong – and I simply can't wait a moment longer to tell you.' Her voice rose. 'It's for ten thousand pounds!'

To this day we do not know who so very, very generously

sent it, or how they could have heard about the Building Fund. However it put up our total to fourteen thousand pounds.

Frances arrived back on Fetlar for the school Easter break. Partly she came to make her final arrangements about moving up to join us in August, and partly because she could not stay away. During this holiday she met and became good friends with Rose, and out of their friendship they decided to apply for one of the empty council houses on the island, with the idea of sharing until we had built enough accommodation to house us all adequately.

Soon after Frances had returned to Worcester, Sybil came up to spend a few more days with Mimie, and it was whilst she was with us all that she told me that on the strength of having solved the problem that she had asked us to pray about, she could now give us a cheque for five thousand pounds.

Knocking in the last nail I step back, hammer in hand, and survey the job that has taken me two whole days to achieve. Yes, I feel quite pleased, though there's still a lot of room for improvement, an improvement that can only come, unfortunately, with money. The walls, cracked and damp, let in buckets of water during the winter and the wind that comes through the cracks, too, will probably prohibit our using the little room at that time of the year. However, it should make a darling chapel and I can hardly wait for the community to see it. I've certainly been meaning to have a go at the job since I first poked my head around the door and saw it as a challenge.

I am over at Da Gaets, where I've come to have a few days of space and thinking time. So often, when I need refreshment of soul and yet need to use my mind, I find that it helps to use my body too, to achieve the best results. It is, I believe, a form of prayer practised through a process of using one's whole person, an ancient method used in both the Eastern and Western Churches. We in the west still use it in the saying of the Rosary, and I'm told that in the East, centuries ago, a person praying would often similarly use a small mound of stones, moving the stones one by one from one side of

108

himself to the other and at the same time recite his prayers. The idea was, that with the mind and the body occupied, the soul was set free to praise God. For myself, I find this true in the sense that I often experience a lovely feeling of release and inspiration whilst working physically and mentally at the same time. Or could one call it procrastination of sitting down at the word processor?

This is how I have started my writing retreat, then, by clearing out the old porch and turning it into a tiny chapel. My family on Fetlar will laugh knowingly when they hear what I've done, and will accuse me of never being so happy as when I've a hammer in my hand.

It has taken me one of these two days to sort out the years of clutter that folk have pushed into this porch, and then to emulsion the walls. This done, I then started the creative part of the job. What fun I've had, finding the bits and pieces of wood to make the tiny pews, altar and a wooden cross. As Da Gaets means The Way, now that it's finished I think that we must name this small sanctuary The Way Chapel. How special a place it is with the pews polished, a piece of old blue matting on the floor and two pots of flowers on the altar under the cross. The small window, its surrounds now painted white, looks out over the valley which runs down to the sea. This will be for me, I know, a great source of meditation . . . I must tear myself away and as soon as I've washed and changed out of my working clothes I'll return, have some prayer time and say Vespers.

Soon back, I'm at the stage now of saying Office. It's the sabbath tomorrow and the service is the First Vespers of Good Shepherd Sunday. Suddenly, as I mark my places in the breviary, it's occurred to me, and with such pleasure, that this service will commemorate the seventh anniversary of the first Office that Rosemary and I ever said in the oratory at The Ness. The oratory is dedicated to Jesus the Good Shepherd and, joy of joys how appropriate, not only was this Vesper service for that occasion but also for this first service I'm going to say now:

> I am the Shepherd
> of the sheep, I am the Way, the truth,
> and the life: I am the Good Shepherd,
> and know my sheep, and am known of mine.
> Alleluia. Alleluia.[2]

11 Rise to the Clouds

One night, as summer was approaching, I woke up in the early hours with the uncomfortable feeling that something was wrong. Drowsily, trying to push away a terrible ache, I twisted myself around on to my other side and . . . Ouch! An excruciating pain stabbed me in my neck, my left shoulder and down my left arm. Mystified, I levered myself up a fraction, hoping that a sitting position would ease the discomfort. Alas, to no avail. I flopped back with a shudder of surprise and at that moment Sister Mary Clare's light down in the ben room clicked on. What a relief it seemed, yet because of my pain I did not feel at all equal even to calling out. Lying a second or so I thought, then, stretching out my good arm, I managed to switch on the bedside light. Maybe she would see it and call upstairs to see if all was well. Her door squeaked open, there was a pad, pad of her slippers and then a silence. After that, there seemed an eternity of waiting and stretching my ears until, joy, I heard the sound of her return. Perhaps this time, she would see my light and wonder why it was on. Ah, now she had stopped and I could hear whispering. It must be to Tildy, or one of our feline friends . . . 'Please God, let her come,' I prayed. Then, with the hard click of finality, her door closed. By this time I knew that I had to find help – get to her somehow. Slowly, with sweat streaming from my brow, I crawled out of bed, down the stairs and pushed open her door. She was out of bed in a flash.

'What is it?' she gasped.

'I'm not sure . . .' I whispered, 'but my back is killing me.'

She took hold of my doubled-up frame and half dragged, half lifted me on to her bed. 'I won't be a minute,' she promised, pulling her duvet around me. 'I'm going to put on the kettle for a hot bottle to lay against your back.' Bless her, she returned in a jiffy, and although the warmth of the bottle did not take away much of the pain it was a comfort. 'Would you like me to ring the nurse now, or can you wait for just another hour or so, until she's up?'

'I'll wait . . . Please don't disturb her. What d'you think's wrong with me?'

'I would think that you've a badly trapped nerve in your spine and that the nurse will give you something to ease the pain. Is it still hurting?'

'Mmm, but the bottle's nice, thank you.'

'OK, I'll get one of the seats off the old studio couch for myself and lay it on the floor by the side of you. I'll only snooze, so call if you need me.'

Listening to Sister Mary Clare lugging and pushing the long piece of seating and knowing that she, too, had a back problem, I felt, almost for the first time in my life, frustratedly helpless. However, in due course, she settled it by the side of my bed and in two shakes was herself tucked up and, yes, snoring. Setting myself to accept the pain, I whiled away the time trying to pray for all those in a worse state than myself, knowing that there were millions. At about 6.30 a.m. Sister Mary Clare arose and rang the nurse, who kindly said that she would come at once.

'Now, what have you been up to?' asked the nurse in a kindly way. I brightened, for her presence was reassuring. 'I want to see where exactly the pain's catching you. Could you take my arm?' She tested the movements in each of my arms; the left one was still numb though I could move it. Then she explained that she was going to ease me up into a sitting position very slowly. No sooner had she started than I winced aloud and she set me back. 'Have a rest, Sister, and we'll try again.'

Twice we tried and the third time she held me upright. 'Sister Mary Clare,' she called, 'could you possibly bring us a glass of milk?' With the milk she handed me a couple of red pills then gently, very gently, lowered me back into the pillow. 'We're going to have to send you to Lerwick for an x-ray as soon as you can manage it,' she smiled. 'Meanwhile, the pills will ease the pain and when they have, try to get some sleep. You could have a trapped nerve, though I'd like to be certain.

I'll come around later in the day to see how you are and I'll bring you a sling which will help the arm.'

Everyone was kind, and gradually, as nurse had said, the pain eased. I continued to take the anti-inflammatory pills and within a fortnight, feeling much better, was called to Lerwick for an x-ray.

Another couple of weeks elapsed until late one afternoon the telephone rang. 'The x-ray results have arrived,' the nurse told me. 'You've something called cervical spondylosis, which is a degenerative condition, so you'll have to be careful not to lift heavy weights and therefore will need to cut out some of those hefty jobs you're so fond of doing.' She explained that part of a disc in my spine had worn away and because of this, a nerve had subsequently been trapped, so causing the pain.

'Bother,' I complained, and sighed. It rather looked as though my happy lifestyle was going to have to take on a new look. What a good thing that I had the others to help.

About the same time that my back problems began, Rose was given the key to Number Seven Stakkafletts. Number Seven was a nice house and approximately one and a half miles from The Ness. During her days off from the hospital each week, which she spent on Fetlar, she worked many an hour in the house, scrubbing and decorating it. Frances was due to arrive with her furniture at the end of the summer and there was still much to be done in preparation. Sister Mary Clare, Rosemary and I went over on one particular evening to help, taking brooms and mops and dusters, and wound up our working hours tired and happy by saying our Office of Compline, each sitting on a bare board of the stairs, this being the only seating that we had. A lighted candle was placed on the corner of the bannister rail to give the right atmosphere. We thought that this was probably the first time that the little house had ever had a service held in it.

As far as our own building project was concerned, plans were coming off the drawing board fast and furious. So one day we journeyed into Lerwick to introduce ourselves to Stephen Johnson, Ned's quantity surveyor friend, and to present to him our ideas.

'You should make a start,' he announced, having listened to our tale. 'You say that you've fourteen thousand pounds?'

'Yes,' we nodded, 'though what can we do for that amount of money?'

'Quite a lot! To start with, you should get the site levelled and then have a site survey done. That will put you in a much better position to ascertain what kind of building you want and indeed, can afford.'

We talked to Stephen for some time and listened to his sound advice. 'So,' I said, 'you think that the best plan would be to start now, rather than waiting around until we've raised the rest of the money?'

'Definitely. The rest of the money is far more likely to come if you make a start. I imagine you'd be aiming at fifty thousand, maybe a little more?'

'It sounds an awful lot of money,' we said, feeling somewhat stunned by the figure, and stood to make our farewell.

'Yes, it is, Sisters, yet I've a feeling you'll raise it.'

'We shall, certainly, if we're meant to . . . Anyhow, thank you, Stephen, enormously, and yes, we'll do exactly that – make a start.'

Visitors, mostly unexpected ones, poured in over the next few weeks and I gave great thanks to God for sending me Sister Mary Clare. She is by nature a delightful hostess and wonderful cook, usually accomplishing both these jobs with little effort. Most especially, though, I was grateful for her presence over the late summer when I began to feel under the weather again with a trying bladder problem. This persisted for two months and was an absolutely unheard-of state of affairs for me, who had always been so healthy. Also, added to the problem diagnosed in the top of my spine, a sharp pain in my left hip was also causing me trouble. As if all this were not enough, I found, aggravatingly, that I, who had always been so skinny, had begun to put on weight. Having shot up from barely eight stone to ten almost overnight, I felt that middle age was beginning to take its toll!

Our island nurse was concerned that the lower back trouble might be a slipped disc and took the precaution of making me lie flat until the doctor visited the island on his fortnightly visit. Rose was working in Lerwick at the time, Rosemary away on her annual around-Britain trek and Frances had not yet arrived.

All this meant that poor Sister Mary Clare was run off her feet, for a whole fleet of visitors arrived, including Di and Sándor, friends of ours from Fife, with four of their daughters, to camp, as they usually did, in Rosemary's garden. Also two other folk, one a lady from Midlothian and the other a young Shetland housewife, each rang up with an SOS. Could we have them to stay? There were reasons in both cases why we should, so with Sister Mary Clare making encouraging noises at me to allow her to say yes, how could I say no? In the midst of all this Frances, with her daughter Jenny, who had come to help her mother settle in at Number Seven, arrived from Worcester with a household of furniture. Or rather, *without* her household of furniture, at least to start with!

By this time I was just out of my bed, having seen the doctor who was sure that my hip trouble was nothing to do with a disc at all. Slightly puzzled, he had suggested that he review the problem when I had had a course of physiotherapy. This meant that I was up and hobbling around on the day of the great arrival, and I insisted upon going down to the ferry with Sister Mary Clare to meet them. They rolled off the boat in Frances' secondhand 'Yellow Peril', as we call it, a small, sturdy, knocked-about little car. They waved with gusto and we waited for a large furniture van to follow them off. Several cars came off, and a crowd of people, yet there was no sign of van . . .

'Welcome, welcome!' we cried as they drew up alongside us and there were smiles and hugs. 'But Frances, where's your furniture?'

'I haven't the slightest idea,' she laughed. She was glowing with the pleasure of having arrived and nothing, not even the loss of three furniture vans, would have quenched her exuberance. 'We lost the van somewhere in Aberdeen. Perhaps I could use your phone and make a few inquiries later.'

'Of course, Frances, but meanwhile let's all get back to The Ness and have some coffee,' I encouraged.

After coffee and a jolly lunch together, Frances rang around and discovered that her furniture van had, in fact, arrived in Lerwick and was hoping to reach Fetlar by the late afternoon. This it managed to do and the men unloaded it amazingly quickly. This may have been because they were hoping to catch the last ferry out of Fetlar that day, which gave them two hours to do the job. Or it may just have had something to do with the clouds of midges which were fiercely interested in a glut of new blood from the south.

Our two emergency visitors arrived, and what nice women they were, though how much they both needed to relax. The Shetland wife, Glynda, was a young English girl who had lived most of her short married life with an invalid husband. She kept goats and chickens around their croft home on the Shetland Mainland and had the usual dog and cat. 'I need time and space to think and pray and just be myself without any external pressures being made upon me at all,' she explained. 'Sisters, I'm so grateful you said yes.'

We accommodated her in the big caravan which she loved, and Margaret, our other guest, we installed in Rose's small one. Each of them shared our main meal of the day and came to join in with whatever Offices they wished. After only three days Glynda looked a different woman and literally went away singing. In fact, she had brought her guitar along with her and whilst whiling away time on her own, had composed one of her beautiful little songs. She had used the inspiration of a piece of Scripture and the words and music told of the love, glory and joy of God. On her last evening she asked if she could sing, not this one, but another of her compositions at Compline:

> I am the God of all comfort
> And I will comfort you.
> I am the God of all comfort
> And I will comfort you.

All those disappointments
Yes, I know how you feel:
Misunderstood and rejected,
I have experienced it all.

And I am the God of all comfort
I will comfort you.
And I am the God of all comfort
I will comfort you.

So do not turn away now
And struggle on your own,
To the weary and heavy-laden
I will give my rest

If you come to me
The God of all comfort
And let me comfort you.
Come to me, the God of all comfort
And let me comfort you.

I am the God of all comfort
Let me comfort you.

There was no doubt that Glynda had been refreshed, as indeed
was our other friend Margaret, though in an entirely different
manner. Margaret experienced something that she would
never in a hundred years have expected, on an island such as
Fetlar.

Frances, who is a gifted and enthusiastic handbell ringer,
is the proud possessor of a beautiful set of bells. Naturally,
she likes to practise and enjoy her skill, though this of
course requires that she enlists the help of a team. With
regard to this, she has also learned another art, the art of
recruitment . . . Beware, then, if ever you are invited to her
house for tea! The first time that this spider-and-fly drama
happened to us (and on this occasion it included Margaret,
too) was at the house-warming party which Frances and

Jenny gave as soon as Number Seven Stakkafletts looked reasonably like home. There we were, having enjoyed a lovely tea, feeling replete and about to depart. Suddenly, and we hardly know how, we found ourselves with a bell in each hand and a piece of music on our knees. Could this manipulative piece of strategy have been worked out by our quiet, gentle Frances? I mused. Surely not! For planned it must have been, a tactic of this proportion, which not only included Margaret and ourselves but also a couple of holiday makers who were staying on Fetlar. Frances had met them on the ship when travelling up and had invited them to call in at some point. When the poor innocents knocked on the door at an appointed moment they were lured inside, to 'make up numbers'. It was great fun and was the first of many happy hours that we have had as a group, handbell ringing; though some of us are still not wonderfully proficient. Margaret thoroughly enjoyed it and laughed louder than any of us at our ridiculous blunders.

Margaret and Glynda may have benefited from their stay with us, yet we, in turn, benefited from our receiving of these two women, for suddenly, through our encounter with them, a whole new dimension of life and its possibilities presented itself to us: we saw that we must allow a small corner of this paradise which God had given to us for such people as these, with their kind of need – the need for freedom.

'You know, Sister, the caravan won't last for ever and it's been such a marvellous place for our visitors,' said Sister Mary Clare to me one day. 'When we do eventually build, d'you think we might consider perhaps including two small chalet units as part of the project? Something about the same size as the caravan, yet something that's strong and weatherproof and which could be a refuge for people during the spring and autumn, and even in the winter months of the year too, instead of only in summer.'

'It's worth considering,' I assented, 'though we'll have to apply to the Lord for extra funds.'

We thought more and more about it and the more we thought, the more we liked the idea. Needless to say we came decidedly to the conclusion that, if it were meant, we would be shown ways to bring it about.

We kept closely in touch with both Margaret and Glynda and heard in the process much more about Glynda's Golden Guernsey goats.

'Ooh, I'd love a goat . . .'

'No, no goats,' I said. 'Reason number one, Sister Mary Clare, is that we can't afford more animals since we already have four cats and a dog. Reason number two, a goat would take up more time than we can afford at the moment; and reason number three, I've always been of the opinion that they're completely overrated, since they'll eat everything in sight and jump any wall or fence to get at it. They'll even have a chew at the washing hanging on the line if they're given a chance. No, no goats . . . and another thing, they don't have waterproof coats so we would constantly be moving the creature under cover whenever it rained.'

Sister Mary Clare, downcast, did not argue. However, later that evening I could not help hearing a murmur about the fact that a kid would have made a very nice fiftieth birthday present.

'I heard,' I responded, 'and Religious don't keep birthdays.'

'Not even fiftieth ones in a community that's a little different?'

'I doubt it,' I smiled, making a mental note that I would, when I was in on my own some time, ring Glynda and see what she thought.

The painful discomfort in my hip and spine, along with my bladder problem, continued and after various consultations with the doctor I was sent to the hospital in Lerwick for a scan. Sister Mary Clare travelled the sixty miles with me since I only drove on a provisional licence. This conveniently allowed me to drive without a qualified driver beside me on the three most northerly islands of Shetland, which is what I mostly do, though not on the Shetland Mainland. I had passed my driving test at the age of seventeen but had given it up on entering the Franciscan Order.

We arrived at the hospital in good time and asked directions through what seemed to us to be a maze of corridors. 'You'll need to go upstairs, to the scanner in the maternity unit today, dear,' I was told. 'Doctor will come up when he's ready.'

'Maternity unit?' I gasped.

Sister Mary Clare stifled her laughter. 'Come on, it'll be all right,' she encouraged in an infuriatingly worldly-wise manner.

We arrived somewhat breathless as a nursing sister came briskly towards us from a corridor at the top of the stairs. A quirky look of surprise flickered across her face as I asked about the scanner. 'Do come this way and I'll show you where to sit and wait,' she proffered and we followed her up the wide passage alongside a ward of young women with babies.

We had each brought a book with us to read, though I found my concentration was registering zero and my face was growing redder at the arrival of each rotund expectant mother who squeezed herself on to a chair in the waiting area beside us. Sister Mary Clare seemed as oblivious to everything except her book as the expectant mum who sat opposite flicking the pages of a baby care magazine to and fro. She looked no more than a child herself, I thought. 'Isn't this a lovely one, Frank?' she asked, nudging the slightly bored youth beside her. 'Or do you like this colour better? Just a minute, I'll show you another set.' Licking a forefinger, she swept more rustling pages across the disinfectant-laden silence which merged suddenly into a crack of footsteps coming down the corridor in our direction. It was the sister.

'Sister Agnes?' she called, and looking along the row of faces, stopped at me.

'Yes, I'm Sister Agnes,' I admitted weakly.

'Doctor is waiting to see you in the scanner room downstairs.'

Relief welled through me and in a voice that everyone could hear I said, 'Oh yes, we thought that perhaps we had been directed to the *wrong department*.'

The scan showed an ovarian cyst. 'Look, there it is, can you see it?' the doctor asked, turning the scanner screen in my prostrated direction.

'I'm not sure that I really want to. Oh, all right,' I said, peering timidly over my right shoulder. To my surprise the screen did not show me the intimate details of my abdomen that I was expecting. Instead, there was nothing more than an unrecognisable blur, at least to an untrained eye.

He pointed a finger towards what seemed to be a darker piece of cloud on the screen. 'This area,' he said kindly, tracing an outline around it.

'It looks quite large. Is it?' I asked.

'I've seen much larger,' he answered.

'Will it mean an operation?'

'Yes, could do.'

The scan was later followed up by another trip to Lerwick to see the hospital's visiting gynaecologist. This was not at all a pleasant experience and resulted in the surgeon telling me that he would have me in Aberdeen within a fortnight. The real healthy me would have been horrified to have been told that I needed to go to hospital in Aberdeen since it meant leaving my home in Shetland for a while. However, my only feeling at that moment was one of instant relief; at last, something was going to be done.

As the fortnight passed, I felt increasingly ill and when after ten days we had still not heard anything, and various arrangements were needing to be made at the Fetlar end, Sister Mary Clare rang the hospital. She was at once put through to the ward where, by an enormous fluke, the surgeon was doing his rounds. Since she had once been the wife of a gynaecologist herself, she knew the right things to ask.

The surgeon was very kindly. 'You ought to get a letter tomorrow, saying that she's to be admitted on Monday,' he told her.

'In that case, I'm glad that I rang because, living on a remote island, our next post isn't until Monday afternoon. Also, it takes half a day to get to the ship from here, after which, as you know, there's a fourteen-hour voyage . . . We'll need to get on to booking our tickets at once. How long is she likely to be in hospital?'

He explained that since there was a 'mass', as he called it, we could reckon that I would be in for roughly three weeks.

By the time that Sister came off the phone she was worried, though she hid it in a matter-of-fact manner. 'Now, no more arguments about going on your own. I'm going with you. Frances will move into The Ness and look after the animals and I'll take a lot of work with me to get on with, for when I'm not visiting.' There was nothing else to be said. Sister Mary Clare had taken command.

Our friends the Episcopalian Sisters of the Society of St Margaret were only too pleased to accommodate my carer, and me too if necessary, and offered us the use of their little holiday cottage on the outskirts of Aberdeen for my convalescence afterwards. That evening Sister set the sewing machine on the but room table and quickly ran me up two lovely new nighties with some material that we had bought for that purpose weeks before.

'I'm not visiting you in hospital looking quite as Franciscan as you do in your old night wear,' she told me, and I was too ill to demur.

I unhitch the bell rope and clasp it in my right hand, tugging it to and fro carefully, yet firmly. The clapper falls heavily against the bell's great belly and so reverberates a peal of hopefulness over the isle. Three times three I ring, with a pause for prayer at the end of each triplet. I listen to the murmur of voices through the open byre/chapel door and I too move my lips, saying the familiar words. Now, as I prepare to ring out the last long toll of the final Collect, my eyes automatically peer, as they always do, across the potato rig and on, up, over the fields into the distance. There, I'm conscious of an empty road where, so often in the past when it has been my turn to ring the Angelus, I've seen Anthony's car winding along it. Now it lies empty . . .

Anthony was always everywhere, or so it seemed. Digging ditches, gritting the road, checking it for repairs and in between this regular island job of his, giving a hand to anyone who could be doing with the assistance of a strong young man. In and out of the homes of us all, he was well liked, as friend or relative. Certainly he'd helped me with many a heavy job around The Ness and always in a kindly way. Together, we'd laid a piece of hard-core road so that the car could be parked without the bother of churning the grassy parking place into a winter mud bath. He'd also, on a second occasion, brought along a load or two of hard-core for the site for Rose's caravan. On many other occasions he'd driven down to The Ness to make sure all was well and often had insisted upon helping me out with mending a gate or a piece of fence. He'd helped the haulage carrier too, to unload the 'big caravan' off the truck when it had arrived. And once, when I was struggling to erect two metal clothes poles, he not only came to the rescue and cemented them in for me but returned the following day with a clothes prop that he had made, as a gift.

With one more jerk, I ring out a final boom and now, hitching the bell rope back into its place, I turn towards the chapel. Anthony will never be seen on his tractor, with his shovel, or in his motor car, again.

It happened in this way, Anthony had an accident, a terrible accident. He'd fallen from a piece of cliff on his croft, where only his tractor, its engine still running, could hint of his whereabouts. For days, helicopters and divers searched until at last, sadly, his body was recovered from the sea. The whole isle, shocked to its core, almost stopped breathing. A great blanket of gloom was cast about it, a gloom that could hardly be penetrated. Pain was in every face and death in the forefront of every mind.

I close the chapel door behind me and lift all thoughts of our friend to God, knowing beyond doubt that all is well and cannot be otherwise. We, as a community, have each individually experienced pain and loss and have had to face up to the fear of death, and we know that it can and should be a positive source of joy. 'Therefore with joy', says Isaiah, 'shall ye draw water out of the wells of salvation.'[1] Water, or shall we call it life? Water, that bubbles up and flows over.

The rough wood of my stall is comforting. I kneel and the Office commences with the opening prayers, the Psalms, the Little Chapter, the hymn and now the versicle and responsory of the day:

V. Thou Lord, hast turned my mourning into joy, alleluia.

R. Thou hast destroyed my heaviness and surrounded me with joy, alleluia.[2]

12 *Wings of Love*

All set, the car loaded, and ready to say our sad farewells, we drank in our last draught of home. We had added on three extra weeks for convalescence after my hospital stay, which meant six long weeks away. Six weeks seemed an eternity and I hardly dared think of it. Frances very nobly had moved into The Ness to answer the telephone, cope with callers and look after Skerry, Flugga, Mooskit and Tildy.

We set off with Sister Mary Clare at the wheel and the car piled high, mostly with sewing jobs for her to work at whilst we were away. 'Everything except the kitchen sink' just about described it. We had a sewing machine, a part roll of tweed with which to make new scapulars, a typewriter, all sorts of bits and pieces of mending that there never seemed time to do at home, and a whole lot of craft work items to sort out and work at. Added to this there were books to read, two travelling bags carrying personal necessities, a various assortment of plastic bags, gum boots, mackintoshes and – the most important item of all – Sister Mary Clare's pillows. Because of her neck problem the pillows have to travel with her wherever she goes.

'Since we have to take the car with us,' said Sister Mary Clare (the car, by the way, was the third-hand Volvo that she had brought to Fetlar with her when she joined me), 'then I may as well fill it up with something to do.' I smiled, for it is always the same, even on a trip to Yell for the day – she has an ingrown, strongly rooted habit of filling the car up, 'in case of . . .'

On our arrival in Lerwick we went straight along to St Magnus' church where we had arranged to meet Father Lewis, and there he heard my confession and gave me his blessing. It was the loveliest send-off I could possibly have had, except that it made everything seem rather more solemn.

We had been advised, under the circumstances, especially with the bladder problems, that we should book a cabin on the

St Clair with toilet and wash basin facilities. Unfortunately, the only one available at so late a date of booking, was up front in the prow. 'Isn't it super,' we said to each other when we first saw it . . . Little did we know!

'A porthole! . . . Look, we can see all sorts of things happening on the quay, and what a lovely angle it gives on the town.'

'What about going along to the restaurant now and having a bite of supper? Or would you like to wait until later?' asked Sister Mary Clare.

'If you don't mind, I'd like to lie down for half an hour and then see . . . perhaps go along later, just for a snack, something very light. You have an adequate supper though, Sister, you deserve it after the long drive and all our traipsing around.'

'In that case I think I'll have forty winks first myself,' she said and flopped down on her bunk. 'Sweet dreams . . .'

'Sweet dreams,' I answered snoozily, but at that moment . . . Clank . . . Whirr . . . Bang . . . Thud. Bang, thud. Bang, thud. Bang, thud. Clatter, clonk, clatter, clonk. The row was so loud that we could only mouth at each other across the cabin and stick our fingers in our ears. The whole ship seemed to be shaking to pieces. Sister Mary Clare came over to me and leaned close enough for us to hear ourselves speak.

'What is it, d'you think? Could it be the anchor being wound up?'

'Yes, that's exactly what it sounds like. Are we sailing yet?'

She looked out through the porthole. 'Yes . . . we're slowly moving out.'

'Hope the racket won't go on all night.'

The racket did go on for quite a while and then, as suddenly as it had started it stopped, and how blissfully silent the world seemed. We were on our way . . . 'Farewell, Shetland,' my heart beat, 'though not for a moment longer than really necessary.'

What a dreadful journey it was, giving us our first experience of sea sickness; I doubt if we shall ever forget it. Normally, I love sailing, though not that night, for the wind whipped up gigantic waves and being in the prow we were heaved up and down, to and fro and simply had to lie flat in our beds to prevent ourselves being thoroughly ill. I, of course was suffering with my bladder, so consequently had to rise frequently to lurch, slither, slip and even resort to crawling across to the toilet. On other occasions I'd always loved the motion of the ship. This time I felt ghastly and did not sleep the whole night. 'Now be sensible,' I remember telling myself, clinging to the sides of the bunk. 'Come on. It's a case of mind over matter . . . and there's absolutely nothing anyone can do to make you feel better anyway. You can't get off for another ten hours, so you'd better just lie still and accept how you feel. Come on, offer your whole being, sickness and all, into the hands of God.'

To start with I lay thinking. Sister Mary Clare, after her talk with the surgeon, had eventually told me that my operation could be a serious one. I was staggered and realised that that accounted for her dark mood. In the end, unable to keep her distress to herself she had wept on my shoulder. 'You won't die on me will you? Please?' She had pleaded. Strangely and wonderfully I had felt in awe over this new possibility and coming quickly to terms with it, was able to comfort her.

'I probably won't, though if that is the case, well, won't that be lovely for me and I know that God will give you and Rosemary, Frances and Rose all the grace, strength and wisdom you need to take SOLI on.'

'We wouldn't, and it's not that – well, not so much, as we'd miss you . . .'

'Yes, it'd be your sorrow that I'd mind most,' I had replied. 'Anyhow, don't let's cross our bridges before we come to them. Come on . . . it may never happen.'

Yet as I was rolled this way and that in my bunk, I had to admit to life's fragility. Death could be around the corner for any of us, I knew, yet if it were for me, and let's face up to it, fairly and squarely – how would I feel? Well, I did not this minute feel any kind of anxiety. No, not at all. Indeed, the strange and lovely thing was that I was more anxious for Sister Mary Clare and the community than for myself. My beloved family in God, I was only too aware, by the very nature of life, especially the Christian life, could expect to be buffeted by many storms. Here was I, at peace in my heart despite the tempest-tossed boat and feeling already wonderfully upheld and cherished by a tremendously strong force all around and within me . . . Yet had I honestly meant it when I told Sister Mary Clare that the community could manage without me? It would certainly grow in a different way . . . Yes, I was a conceited ass, yes, of course they could . . . With God at the tiller, they couldn't go wrong. Wasn't I always quoting to them that 'all things work together for good to them that love God'? . . . I knew that they did, for however terrible a situation is, God will always use it for good if we really trust and love him.

The wind blew steadily into a real gale until every timber of the vessel creaked and groaned. Suddenly, none of this mattered. Metaphorically I took hold of God's hand and let my mind rest in him . . .

The next morning, both of us rather worse for wear, we docked in Aberdeen, where we quickly retrieved the car from the car deck and made our way to the convent. The Sisters had been friends of mine for about six years and it was always a great pleasure to see them. We had a wonderful welcome, along with coffee and biscuits, after which we were shown to Sister Mary Clare's room. Whilst she unpacked, I lay on her bed and snoozed for a while, knowing that I must conserve enough strength to pay our promised visit to the Dean. The Dean of the diocese lived out at Ellon, a village on the outskirts of Aberdeen, a good few miles away, and since I was to be admitted into hospital at three o'clock we needed to get there as soon as possible.

As we drove out of the city a strange wave of vulnerability came over me. In a sense, it was a weird flashback to the way I had felt as a child, when my parents, waving me goodbye, had left me behind in a large, unfamiliar hospital miles from home. How could they have done it, I had felt then, just to have my tonsils and adenoids removed? This same alarming feeling of having all that is comfortable, peaceful, familiar and secure, taken from one, for a moment pricked my heart.

The Dean opened the door of his home to us and with smiles of delight beckoned us into his study. Inside, we chatted over a cup of coffee and a biscuit before being taken over to see his church, which was something that we specially wanted to do.

'It's beautiful, Father,' I said, as he and I approached the sanctuary steps.

'Yes, isn't it,' he said gently, and then more loudly, 'Sisters, shall we say a short prayer?'

The Dean is a quietly-spoken man of prayer, and I felt a sudden strength in him as I dropped into a kneeling position on the sanctuary step.

'Sister Mary Clare,' he beckoned, 'come and stand here and lay one of your hands with mine on Sister's head.'

The warmth of their hands penetrated my scalp in a comforting way and although my discomfort was not instantly relieved as he prayed for my healing, I felt that their combined ministering was of unique value.

Afterwards, the Dean invited us to share a pot of soup with him though, having a second appointment that day with the Chancellor of the Diocese, one of SOLI's trustees, we reluctantly had to decline. However, since (conveniently) the Chancellor's headquarters were also in Ellon, the Dean made another suggestion.

'Look,' he said, 'let me drive you round to Bob's office. It'd save you a lot of time finding him yourselves and then I could bring you back here again when you've seen him. There are several things I could do in the village anyhow whilst waiting, and I'd feel much happier if I knew that you'd had something to eat.'

We succumbed gratefully and had a most enjoyable visit to the Chancellor, who was at that time conveyancing the transaction of the piece of land that had been gifted to us by Andrew and Sheila. Later, the Dean gave us a gorgeous bowl of soup and after this we solemny set off again to Aberdeen.

Sister Mary Clare switched on the engine, released the clutch and, waving to the Dean we glided down his drive and out on to the road. 'We're in good time after all, so let's drive back by the coastal road shall we?'

Looking at my watch I hesitated. 'Mmm, I'd love a last real glimpse of the sea, though . . .'

'Look, Sister, I know that the hospital said you were to be admitted at three o'clock, but from my experience of hospitals I can assure you that they won't be expecting you a minute before teatime. Honestly . . .'

'It would be nice. Right then! Let's go around by the coast.'

We cruised along grassy-edged single-track roads, enjoying the sea, the blue sky, the cotton-wool clouds and the trees. Although we can easily live without them, trees are always a joy and something of a surprise to us when we first arrive back on the British mainland. Breathing more freely I sank back into my seat and savoured to the last drop this extra bonus of time. After a while, Sister Mary Clare pulled in to the side of the road overlooking a field with sheep and cows. There we sat, silently drinking in the scene and thinking our own thoughts.

'Let's listen, softly, to just a bar or two of Grieg on the car cassette,' I suggested, knowing only too well that it would bring the feeling of home nostalgically near. As the strain of our favourite movement died to a close I switched the cassette off. We glanced at each other then silently clasped hands. After a while, hardly daring to break the bond, I turned and smiled at my dear Sister. 'Shall we say our special Celtic prayer together before we go?'

After the usual routine checks on my first afternoon and evening in hospital, I was told that the operation was to be in four days' time. 'There'll be quite a deep cut,' said the young nurse, 'and you'll feel pretty rotten for a while afterwards.'

'I feel pretty rotten now,' I retorted, thinking to myself that I could hardly feel worse. 'In fact, I'm singularly thankful that something's going to be done soon.' The bladder problem and the discomfort from it had become increasingly worse even in the short time since we had left the Dean. 'The Lord obviously didn't have it in mind to heal me that day,' I mused.

The next few days took me through the various motions of preparation until, on the morning before the operation, I was taken down to the hospital's scanning machine for a final update.

The doctor in that department was one of the best in his field, or so I had been told, and he certainly seemed efficient.

Peering at the screen by my right shoulder for what seemed an eternity, at the same time he moved what felt like a round flat instrument across my abdomen. Prostrate on the high narrow bed in the dark room, I was conscious only of the breathing of the man beside me. I waited, until at last . . .

'You'll be pleased to know,' he mumbled, 'that I can't find any thing at all. I've double checked . . . and it's all very strange.'

'It's the Dean's laying on of hands,' was my instant thought.

Later that day the surgeon paid me a visit. 'Sister Agnes,' he said, 'we're mystified. However, I shall still operate tomorrow, though only an exploratory one.

Next morning I was wheeled down to the operating theatre, feeling incredibly calm and cheerful. As I was rattled into the room, the anaesthetist came at once to give me my jab. He bent over me and I remember smiling. At that moment the surgeon, whose voice I could hear, strode into view, apologising and saying that they had just discovered there was a piece of paper that had not been signed and would I mind easing myself up and signing it. I sat up at once, and in such a sprightly manner that the surgeon grinned and a white-coated, younger man chuckled. What seemed like seconds later, having finally been dealt with by the waiting anaesthetist, I was back in the ward in my bed and feeling utterly blotto.

The next day, when the surgeon did his rounds, he told me that all they had found was a polyp in the uterus, which they had removed. 'This means you can leave hospital tomorrow,' he added. A couple of days later my stomach lost its distended look, the discomfort and nausea which I had suffered for weeks disappeared and I stopped having to run to the toilet every half hour.

Since we had taken the car to Aberdeen and because we had earlier had to cancel a much-looked-forward-to holiday on Iona because of my illness, we decided that it might be a good thing to have the holiday after all. We rang home to see how the others felt and all three were enthusiastic and adamant that we should do this and quite prepared to go on holding the fort at Fetlar. So, after two or three days with the Sisters, which allowed me time to surface from all the hospital excitement, we set off.

Suddenly, we felt young again, full of thanksgiving and the inexplicable joys of spring; albeit that this was the end of September with the trees donning their russet dress and some carpeting the earth with thoughts of winter. How blessed we are, was our song, and how privileged – and thank you, thank you, thank you, God . . . we're on our way back to Iona. The drive from Aberdeen to some remote village just this side of Oban was like a dream, which we took gently, so as to savour every moment. Tired and happy I wanted to keep on and on until we arrived, though here Sister Mary Clare drew the line, insisting upon our going bust and staying a night for bed and breakfast en route. Wisely, she would not allow me, intoxicated with joy as I was, to go mad and deprive myself of the rest I still needed. Consequently we stayed at a small place (disturbingly expensive as everywhere seemed to be) surrounded by mountain peaks. Here, once I had recovered from the shock of how much it was going to cost us, I was in the seventh heaven.

A wonderful welcoming party met us at the Iona ferry the next day and trundled us off to Bishop's House where we were to stay for the first few days. After that, as Bishop's House was fully booked, we were transported by our great friend Fiona, the Warden there, over to a darling little cottage called Tighshee, meaning House of Peace. Tighshee was situated on my favourite side of the island and very close to Greenbank. It was owned by a brand new friend of ours, Harold, a retired Presbyterian minister. Harold was a lovely person who, as a thank offering for what Bishop's House had done for him in the way of a kindness, had put himself on their washing-up rota. When hearing, over a sink full of pots and pans one night, that we were looking for accommodation for four or five more days, he immediately offered us his house. After the death of his wife some years earlier he had had a tiny section of their home made into a place where he could live and be independent during the six lighter months of the year. He had done this in order that the rest of the house could be let to summer visitors. Harold's cottage was a glorious place to stay, full of books and very cosy and he made it even cosier for us by insisting upon another kind act. Each morning, usually whilst we were at breakfast, he would knock on the door, come in and then quietly clear and reset the fire for us. A humble act of a humble man.

A little way from Harold's cottage, along the single-track road that leads to the machair and which in the summer is lined with wild iris, stood the home of Bruce, an old friend of Rosemary and me from our visit to Iona in 1976. In fact, as those who have read *A Tide that Sings* will remember, he had ferried us over to the isle in his tiny boat on our arrival. He had described himself then as 'a refugee from Birmingham' and had explained that he and his wife had retired to Iona a short while before and rebuilt a sizeable house called Dun Craig. His wife had now passed away, the large house had been sold and he had built himself a small, rather darling bungalow. At his garden gate, which Sister Mary Clare and I passed often on our walks to the western side of the isle, there was always a wonderful array of boulders and stones. Each was decorated with a beautiful piece of chisel work, and the one that caught my eye time and time again was a large, square-shaped rock, twinkling with mica. On the face of it was a beautiful carving of a Celtic cross.

'Isn't it lovely?' I breathed, as one day we stopped to gaze at it yet again. 'It's far too expensive for us though . . . D'you think we'd be justified in treating ourselves, Sister Mary Clare? It would be a wonderfully tangible sign of the fulfilment of God's promise to me fourteen years ago wouldn't it? Shall we, or is it too terribly wrong and greedy?'

'Look, this is about the first time that I've ever known you want to buy anything and it's your birthday next week . . . Oh yes, I know that we don't officially keep birthdays but I think that on this occasion and for the reason you've just given me, we should. Yes, we'll go and see Bruce after lunch and purchase it.'

'Thank you, that makes me feel a lot easier. And it was Bruce, of course, through whom my call was confirmed to come to the Isles all those years ago . . .' I remember it so clearly: 'Sister Agnes,' he said, 'why don't you come and live here? If them down at the abbey can rebuild, then why don't you come and rebuild the nunnery?' I didn't tell him, or Rosemary, or anyone, until years later that the night before this incident God had seemed to be speaking to my heart, asking me Himself to come north, to come and bring the religious life back to the Scottish Isles. I was awe-struck, though at the same time couldn't help feeling that it was simply wishful thinking, for I was captivated by the isle. However, when saying my morning prayers, impatient to understand, I asked God, in an impetuous manner, to show me the truth. 'If this is really You asking me to do this wonderful thing, then please, God, show me. Show me by some sign,' I cried out. 'I don't like asking for a sign, yet you must understand that I need to know the truth. Look, I know if it's really Your will and not mine, then let an islander invite me to come and live here; and because I must know soon, let them do so before we leave.' Since there was only a couple of days to go before we left I thought that there was only a million-to-one chance that this could happen. So what a surprise it was, when less than two hours later I received Bruce's invitation!

Sister Mary Clare called in to see Bruce later that day. She found that he had his sister staying with him and they very kindly invited us both to tea the next day. Rather wonderfully, though we had not at all planned it like that, it was the fourteenth anniversay of his ferrying of Rosemary and me across to the isle.

So, Bruce it was who had confirmed my call and now, as we carried away that stone to incorporate into our new chapel which, one day, would be built on Fetlar, he it was through whom God ratified it.

It's a much colder autumn day than I imagined when surveying it from the but room window an hour ago. For out here on the headland, although the sun is bright, there are strong whispers of wintertime in the wind. It was silly of me to have come out without something warmer over my navy blue cords and fisherman's smock. A sudden whirl of wind is whisking and snatching the blue scarf around my head and now dashes it back to obliterate my headband.

Quickly, I must survey the scene and return to the house. So as I drink in my last long memory of this breathtaking site, I know full well that in the future I will often remember it as it is today, without buildings, spread around me, green, rock-strewn and dotted with sheep. Its contours slope downwards towards the sea on the south and west sides, down to the Ness burn on the east and across flat and slightly boggy land northwards to The Ness. Tomorrow, the diggers will arrive and after that it'll never look the same again . . .

Nevertheless, I'm convinced that it has been given us by God . . . Thoughts of Him swing me back fourteen years to Iona, and reliving that call to bring the religious life back to the Isles, I can feel the same wind and sun in my face, hear the cry of the gulls and the inflections in Bruce's voice. 'Why don't you rebuild . . . rebuild . . .?' Yes, it was on such an October morning as this that he invited me to do just that. What I didn't know at the time, and what I've since found interesting, is that Bruce himself was a builder!

Reaching out to the Creator of all truth and wisdom, I seek the understanding and knowledge of what is real and what is not. 'I'm a creator too, Lord,' I hear myself saying, 'and I love the medium of stone . . . yet I'm not trained in the art of building. I'm not a St Francis to whom you said, "Go build my church." Oh yes, I've enough imagination to be able to envisage what could be erected here. The whole concept is one of simplicity. The chapel's to be built upon simple lines . . . with a feeling of space and wholeness and full of the presence of God. I can hear music too . . . Lark song, the song of love, plainsong and the strains of an organ. Yes, and the Iona stone will have a prominent, central place, incorporated perhaps into the altar. The altar of Him who will be our rock, our "chief cornerstone", and who, so long ago, was rejected by the builders.'

Am I then a builder after all? In part, perhaps, though only a tiny, tiny part. It's God who is the great master builder, and for Him we, like Christ, are as living stones. 'Ye also as lively stones, are built up into a spiritual house.'[1]

Dear house of SOLI . . . There are five of us now on Fetlar, plus thirty other souls attached to us as family who live further afield.

As well there are a number of women waiting and hoping at the end of a period of time to join us. Are we then . . . I pray so . . . being built up as living stones into a spiritual house?

> God bless the house,
> From site to stay,
> From beam to wall,
> From end to end,
> From ridge to basement,
> From balk to roof tree,
> From found to summit,
>   Found to summit.

I for IRIS and IONA

13 Flight Patterns

Although my abdominal problems had all cleared up and although it was wonderful to be back on Iona I was still, disappointingly, having a lot of pain in my hip. Sister Mary Clare, more concerned about it than I, had a secret talk with our retired doctor friend Nancy, who had bought Greenbank, the little house in which I had first stayed. There, in Nancy's sitting room, they had discussed the pros and cons.

'I would advise you,' Nancy had suggested, 'to get in touch with Sister Agnes' surgeon before you return home. Once in Shetland, as you know, you'll have to go through all the motions of getting back to Aberdeen and there'll be appointments and waiting lists and so on. Ring him now, use my phone if you like, and see what he says.'

'Mmm, yes, good idea, though I'll have to ask Sister Agnes first whether she agrees . . .' After a tussle with me, which she won, Sister Mary Clare returned to Nancy's and got straight through to the surgeon. He promised to readmit me on our way back through Aberdeen and have me transferred to an orthopaedic colleague. So it was, that a few days later, back in Aberdeen, I was x-rayed, laid out on a bed and tapped here and there with a little hammer to test my reflexes. Then I was told that I had arthritis in the bottom of my spine. 'Just what I want,' I complained, 'spondylosis in the top, and arthritis in the bottom.'

'The best thing I can recommend,' advised the surgeon, before he swished away, 'is to swim for an hour every day.'

'Thank you so much,' I said, already feeling the grip of the Shetland waters rising around my neck. 'Thanks a lot . . .'

The next day, before we left Aberdeen, we went into town and bought a swimsuit. In fact we bought two swimsuits – I was not going to suffer this one on my own. Poor Sister Mary Clare – it was unfair revenge.

Soon after our return home the contractor from Yell arrived with his equipment to level the site. This included a giant JCB

135

digger, which looked like some huge prehistoric monster out on the headland. It thumped and thudded, flinging up rocks and mountains of earth until after about ten days two gigantic lorries arrived to accompany it and proceeded to drive to and from the Fetlar quarry, loaded with hard-core which they deposited between The Ness and the new site. In no time at all this was tumbled into a road. It was thrilling, if deafening, to watch, and I for one could hardly believe the miracle that was happening. Again and again I looked at Bruce's Iona rock and heard our crofting friend Andrew saying, 'If you build over there, you'll certainly be building on rock.' In my mind I saw a small wooden chapel, a little house for no more than four Sisters in vows and some simple form of accommodation for just two or three guests. The wooden structures, strong and Scandinavian in style, would blend perfectly into the landscape and the style of our lives would be something that the simplest soul could relate to.

To my mind there is no lovelier site in the whole world and I think that I shall never cease to give thanks to God for it. From our engineer's site survey it appeared that we were going to be able to erect the buildings at split level, which would add a little more character to the place. This pleased me enormously, for not only could we blend the whole complex into the hillside more naturally but it would enable each window to have a lovely view.

The contractor levelling the site did not at all sympathise with my feelings. Neither was dear Sister Mary Clare, nor the rest of the community, a hundred per cent behind the choice of site. In fact she nudged me once or twice in the hope of moving the whole project sideways a little, to an easier, flatter piece of ground. Alas, I can be stubborn, especially when I have an idea so firmly rooted in my mind as this one, and no amount of wagging of heads will bring forth a change of heart. 'I think one day you'll all thank me profusely for this choice,' I told them doggedly. 'And anyway, the land transaction and the decrofting of the ground have all gone through with the solicitors and the Crofting Commissioners.'

After three weeks the heavy machinery bumbled off down

to Oddsta, from where in due course it was sailed back to Yell. A beautiful silence prevailed, and soaking it in we walked up and down our new right of way, getting used to the feel of the site. Tildy became a wonderful excuse for all the extra amount of exercise.

We looked at the site now with new eyes. The corner that stood higher than the rest would be the ideal place for the chapel, we all thought. Though, oh dear, the thought of battling up to it five times on a dark winter's day in a force ten gale rather put a damper on that notion.

'We could build a covered way up to it,' declared Sister Mary Clare, to whom money is rarely an object.

'That would be tremendously expensive and extravagant and would mean a lot of extra rock blasting,' the rest of us argued. 'Anyhow, let's abandon that idea for the moment and look at our original thoughts of putting the chapel on the lower level. What about over here? Along with the house it would get a superb panoramic view of the sea. Yes, and we could have five long slit windows on its south wall which would give a wonderful, open feeling.'

'I think we should put the two visitors' units up on top,' declared Sister Mary Clare, not to be deterred. 'Now see, Sister, if we had the building L-shaped, it would just fit up here and actually would make each unit more private. Also, a different shape would add more character, as well as giving the visitors a lovely view.'

'What about the wind problem?' one of us asked.

'Not a lot of people would be using them during the winter so the wind problem wouldn't be too much of an objection, would it?'

A lovely idea we all thought, though again, an expensive one. 'Yes, well, let's hold it in the back of our minds, have another look at the site survey and wait to see which way God seems to be pushing us,' was the unanimous decision. Also, we needed to wait and see how and if God was going to help us raise some more money. We had, at that stage, about fifteen thousand pounds.

As autumn began to move into winter, Peter, a civil engineer living and working in Shetland, came along with his colleague Bryan to do a second check on the site. They discovered that there were three large areas of rock which would need to be removed before any sort of building work could go ahead. 'No digger will ever move this,' they announced. 'What you'll need to do is to get in a rock breaker, or even have it blasted. In fact, your architect's plans will need to be changed considerably if you really want to build just here. Also,' said Peter, 'he really needs to be here on the spot, to oversee the work and tie all the loose ends together, and see that everything happens at the right moment.'

Unfortunately it was not possible for Roger our architect to come up to Shetland. So we asked Peter and Bryan if they would be prepared to take on the job of overseeing.

'Well, we're very busy, though we could help.' They looked at each other across the room. 'It'd have to be on one condition, though.'

'What's that?' we echoed.

'That we take on your architect's work too,' said Peter. 'Bryan did some training in an architect's office and could easily draw up your final plans. Personally, we think it very foolish for anyone to have an English architect who naturally knows little about the new Scottish rules and regulations. Now if he were prepared to come up and supervise the work, that would be a different matter, but since he isn't, well, we think you've got some serious thinking to do.'

We were in a quandary. I did not a bit want to sign off our kindly architect who had already done so much work for us and, indeed, had come up with some lovely ideas. On the other hand, and Sister Mary Clare, Rosemary and the rest of the community were quite adamant about this, it would seem to be wiser to have someone 'in the know' supervising the whole project. In the end I was outvoted, so sadly, we rang Roger and explained.

One grey November's morning as we drank our hot coffee after Terce, Sister Mary Clare suddenly flapped down the *Shetland Times* that she was reading, peered over the top and exclaimed, 'Wow! Listen to this!' She proceeded to read us an advertisement for a fleet of caravans to be sold off separately for the incredible price of from twenty to fifty pounds each! 'Apparently, the site needs to be cleared quickly,' she further informed us, 'that's why they're so cheap . . . It says that they range in size, from sixteen to twenty-four feet. Of course, there would be the expense of having it removed from site.'

'Even then,' I added, trying to work it out, 'it wouldn't be extortionate. That's if we were lucky enough to buy one in good condition.'

'We?' shrieked Rosemary. 'Do we really need another?'

'It'd be very useful for workmen to stay in when we start building, especially if we had it down on the new site,' Sister Mary Clare intervened.

'Mmm, I see, and later perhaps,' assented Rosemary, 'it could be blocked in as an outhouse or a shed or something of the sort.'

Frances nodded. 'D'you think it might be a good idea to go off and have a look? Then, if we like it . . . Well, I'd be willing to pay out the fifty pounds or so for it.'

I turned to Frances. 'That's kind of you. Shall we go and see? Hands up who'd like a trip to the Shetland Mainland next week?'

Early one afternoon a few days later three of us, full of high spirits, Sister Mary Clare, Frances and I all set off for the jaunt. By the time that we reached the Mainland, we realised that we had only an hour to spare to find the caravan site, look at the vans and get back in time for the ferry connections. Fortunately, we found the site without too many difficulties and the gentleman who owned it appeared, within a few moments, dangling a handful of keys. Those few moments, however, gave us just enough time to walk quickly around and survey the scene. Even more importantly, to stem our disappointment at the eyesore of it all. The caravans were painted the brightest royal blue and white. Had they been camouflaged in green or dove grey I don't think our horror would have been so great. As it was, *en masse* we noticed at once how bumped and battered they were.

Looking sideways at the expressions on the faces of my two

companions I though that I'd better make a few encouraging noises. 'They're really quite good for the money, don't you think? We couldn't have expected anything better could we?' I did not want them jumping back into the car before the owner had arrived. However, at that moment we heard the roar of his car.

'Would you like to look inside some of them?' he asked.

'Yes please.' I said firmly. I just love challenges and by the end of our inspection we had fallen in love with a particular challenge. It was about twenty-four feet long, had a comfortable furnished sitting-room, a kitchen with a cooker and a fridge, a bathroom with a toilet and space for a bath to be fitted, a double bedroom and a smaller area that would have made an extra bedroom. 'How much is this one?' I asked, thinking that it might be more than the price advertised in the paper.

'Fifty pounds . . . D'ye think ye might like it?' He asked, 'because ye'll need tae mak dy minds up quickly.' He went on to explain that all the vans that had not been sold by the following week would be burned due to a council order.

'Oh that is a shame,' I exclaimed. We got into a little huddle and had a conference of war. 'Let's risk it,' we decided, and looking at our watches we jumped into the car, telling him that we'd be in touch.

'What exactly will you use the caravan for when the workmen have finished with it?' asked Frances, as we dashed back to the ferry in the fading light.

To my utter astonishment, for I had not really thought about it at all until that moment, I found myself telling her that it would make a very pleasant place where both Sisters and visitors could go along and sit. A place where they could enjoy the sea view and have space to talk, either together or privately, and where they could take their knitting or sewing or any sort of craft work and make themselves a cup of tea. It could be a kind of free-for-all sitting-cum-craft-room. 'You see, Frances, we don't really have anywhere that we can keep our craftwork and there are quite a few cupboards in that caravan.' Surprising myself more and more I chattered on, certain that neither Sister Mary Clare nor Frances had a clue that the whole concept had just entered my head. Rosemary, Rose and Frances, I reflected, were all artistically gifted in one way or another and would find a craft room a joy. As for Sister Mary Clare, she was trained in embroidery and needlework and had a tremendous interest in any form of craftwork. She, without hesitation, was thrilled by the notion and at once started to work out how she could pass on some of the skills she had learned to others. 'And you, Sister Agnes,' she pronounced, soon well under steam, 'could design cards and notelets, visitors would love to help with the folding of them and it would all help us to earn a living.' From that moment she helped me cement the idea of the craft workshop into a reality. Though in the end it did not quite turn out as we thought.

Sister Mary Clare rang around one or two hauliers to arrange the transportation of the caravan to Fetlar. Alas, the only firm prepared to come to Fetlar had a mechanical problem with his biggest truck/crane and needed time. The caravan owner gave us the deadline of a fortnight to get it moved and that was where a good idea seemed to fizzle into nothing. We actually kept him waiting longer, and he was incredibly kind and patient with us. However in the end, sadly, having got absolutely nowhere with the hauliers, we had to ring up and tell him to go ahead and get rid of it, a dreadful decision. Nevertheless, the seed of the craft workshop had been sown and out of the ashes of the caravan sprang a new aspect of God's marvellous plan for us. We drew a deep breath and went scurrying back to the drawing board.

The large window in the new craft workshop looks out over the cliffs and across the ocean. We have two comfortable chairs and a couch arranged around it, for it is a lovely place to gravitate to, either for a coffee break, to relax or to do the kind of sewing or knitting or writing that can be done on one's knees. I'm sitting here today with a sketch pad on mine, hoping for some inspiration to illustrate this book.

Usually this light, homely room has all kinds of creativity going on in it, but today Sister Mary Clare and I are the only two members of the community down here. She has her head bent over a piece of intricate tapestry work which she has designed herself as one of a wide selection of samplers. Her idea, which is proving successful, is to inspire others to try their own hand at some type of craft. A craft which can be anything ranging from the very simple, such as cards or painted stones, to something less so, like a Shetland shawl or spinning and weaving. She uses both Celtic and Shetland forms of pattern and encourages others who are gifted, to try design also. Hers, today, is being worked in our own SOLI colours of oatmeal, blue and green with a hint or outline of navy and I am looking forward to seeing the finished result. Increasingly, we are finding that such handwork is proving therapeutically helpful to the many people who come and stay – people often in great need of unwinding.

We are fortunate in as much as each of the members of our community is gifted creatively. Rosemary writes and has greatly encouraged me. Her beautiful book, Columcille, which is a life of St Columba, has been widely read and appreciated. Frances, our musician and organist, is also a very fine knitter and maker of candles. In fact her candles, which are extremely professional, are almost too beautiful to burn. We are hoping to persuade her to put aside modesty and teach others the art. Rose, who is no longer an actual member of the community, though she has remained a close friend, is talented in calligraphy and painting and is a marvellous knitter.

How wonderful it is to have gifts which we can use in God's service, that we can share for His glory and in which we can find fellowship in the creativity of producing. How blessed too we are as a community here on Fetlar, that God has chosen each of us so different and yet so alike, and has woven us together into one of His own unique designs.

> Every web, black, white and fair,
> Roan, dun, checked, and red,
> Give Thy blessing everywhere,
> On every shuttle passing under thread.[1]

14 _Wing Beat_

'What about us applying for one of the five empty Fetlar council houses?' suggested Sister Mary Clare one day. 'Several clergy families as you know, have asked to come . . . and we could
use somewhere like that for the people who want to have a
holiday in Fetlar rather than a retreat kind of quiet time.
They'd be far enough away from us too, not to disturb the
peace and quiet of The Ness. What I mean is, if they have
children or want a livelier, noisier sort of holiday it would be
easier, wouldn't it? We could invite them over here of course,
for the odd meals if we wanted to, and the adults I'm sure
would often join us at Vespers or Compline.'

'Sister Mary Clare, how are we going to afford a council
house seeing that we live mostly on your widow's pension and
half of that goes on feeding the animals?'

'I've worked it all out that it would pay for itself. It'd have
to.'

'I really don't feel enthusiastic.'

'Well, let me arrange to slip into the housing department
and just have a little chat to the officials about the possibilities.
There'd be no obligation and I promise on my honour that I
wouldn't let us in for anything you're not happy about.'

'But, Sister, we've enough to cope with at the moment and I
want people who come here to pay only what they can afford,
not some exorbitant rent. No, we simply mustn't allow ourselves to be turned into a business or to be pressurised with
more people than we can give ourselves out to.'

'We won't be, I promise. To start with, the house is at least a
mile and a half away, and just think what rest and refreshment
it could give to so many extra people.'

'That's what I'm afraid of!'

'Please Sister? As for the money side of things, I think the
Shetland Islands Council will probably be very sympathetic to
the idea and let us have it for quite a low rate.'

'Oh, all right. You're an absolute blight! Slip in and see them, though for goodness' sake just keep in mind that the community's not a money-making proposition.'

She made an appointment to see the Director of Housing the next week during our monthly trip to Lerwick, and the outcome was that the director and her deputy were so enamoured with the idea that they asked if we would be interested in taking on not only one but two of the houses at Stakkafletts. That, however, I did stamp on in no uncertain manner. However, we spoke to the Bishop over the 'phone, and to Father Lewis, about having the one council house and they agreed unanimously that we should. In fact the Bishop was so enthusiastic that he presented us with a subsidy from his discretionary fund some months later to help us pay the first year's rent.

It was a cold November and a claustrophobic amount of decision-making seemed to be closing in on us. I sighed, for some of my precious early ideals of staying simple, seemed to be being squeezed from my grasp. I had envisaged a small group of Sisters in a little croft house living the gospel and following as closely as they could the ideals of the early Franciscans, adapting their Rule to mould in with the life on the island and teaching by their example the values of work and prayer. This, up to a point, had come about, though I had discovered very definitely that no more than two Sisters could be accommodated in a small croft house. Had we been allowed to buy the property and build a couple more rooms on to it, it would have been ideal. However, since our landlord had made it clear that he did not want to sell the house, then we could only assume that Father Lewis' idea of building was the right one. Certainly every door in that direction was opening.

Amazingly, dribbles of money were still coming in for the Building Fund, so much so that, having paid five thousand pounds for the site-levelling job, we found that we still had a clear total of fifteen thousand pounds. Although this seemed enormous bounty to us, those in the building trade shook their heads when they thought of it in terms of erecting a small house and chapel, a double-unit visitors' chalet and now a small craft workshop. We, however, remained singularly undaunted, knowing that if indeed it were meant to be then we need have no anxieties.

One firm of builders, whom we hold in high regard, showed enthusiasm over our plans and gave us a quote on the house and chapel of about sixty-two thousand pounds. Yes, fifteen thousand was a mere drop in the ocean.

Rose was still using Da Gaets as a base from which she could get to the hospital in Lerwick where she worked. However, as the nights drew in and the weather conditions became increasingly treacherous she began to think that travelling all those miles to and from an isolated spot, which could so easily be cut off by snow and ice, was foolish. On top of that, the journey was expensive with regard to wear and tear on car tyres and in petrol consumption. 'I really think that I must try and get lodgings in Lerwick,' she told us. 'I love being out at Da Gaets but am finding it very tiring and time-consuming too.'

Thus Da Gaets was left empty for several months, since the rest of us on Fetlar found it equally impossible to travel there in the winter. The house became damp again through not being lived in, and mousy. Rose, meanwhile, was offered the post of the Fetlar nurse which meant that she would have no need for it during the following winter.

'Look, Sister Mary Clare,' I said one day, 'I know that we pay a mere pittance for Da Gaets, but soon we shall have all kinds of extra expenses with this council house project of yours here on Fetlar. Incidentally, we'll soon have to decide how we're going to furnish it. I'm just wondering whether we're really justified in keeping Da Gaets on? Oh, I know that it's a lovely house to use as a hermitage during the more accessible times of the year, yet we're having to pull our belts in really tight as it is . . . And if we gave up Da Gaets, then we could use the furniture from there for Number One Stakkafletts.' A sadness filled me at the thought of giving up the house, despite it seeming to be the most sensible idea, and Sister Mary Clare remained silent. 'Let's call a meeting about it and see how the other three feel, before we make any rash decisions,' I suggested.

By the time that we had our meeting, with a chance to air

our views and to think more deeply about Da Gaets, I found myself no happier in my heart about giving it up. The general thought that we should do so was mixed, and our unanimous vote in the end was that we should hold on to it for another couple of months, then review the situation again. This was absolutely the right decision as it turned out, for staggeringly, during these two months I received a surprise letter from Chris, our landlady. She wrote to tell me that she felt that she was charging us too much rent at ten pounds a week and would we, from the moment that we received her letter, send only fifteen pounds a month! We could hardly believe it and gratefully accepted that this was the answer. From deep inside I was then, somehow, able to allow my hopes to surface. Hopes that one day, Da Gaets would become another such place as The Ness; the centre of another SOLI wheel.

Soon after this, Rose, as long planned, went off to visit her elderly parents in Australia and on her return gave up her hospital job in order to come and live permanently on Fetlar. She had a month or two to wait before she took up her duties as the island nurse, and she lived happily alongside Frances in Number Seven Stakkafletts.

As usual, during November, our friend Sybil arrived on Fetlar and this time presented us with her promised cheque which had originally been for five thousand pounds. However, having wisely placed it into a high interest account, and having arranged also to give it to us as a one-off covenanted gift (when legally it was possible to do such a thing) it had gained, with interest and with tax reduction, another three thousand pounds. This was astonishing and raised our fund to twenty-three thousand pounds. Yes, things were really beginning to move, and all manner of people, including the media, were suddenly interested.

It was around this time that I had a telephone call from a young lady asking for some information about our Building Project. At first I adamantly dug in my heels, declaring that I did not wish to answer questions, though as she continued to chat, gradually I felt a sincerity, warmth and sensitivity come through. In the end we had a surprisingly lengthy discussion about the plans and Sister Mary Clare beamed as I put down the receiver.

'Well done.'

'What about?' I glared. I knew that she was aware of my aversion to journalists, though actually some of our nicest friends are media people.

'You did tremendously well,' she laughed. 'No doubt she'll write a super article and hundreds of pounds will come in for the fund.'

Grimacing at her I sat back at the but room table and picked up my pen. At that time we were in touch with about five hundred people over Christmas and the New Year, and already cards, letters and parcels were piling in.

A couple of days later, flipping through a bundle of post before lunch, I pulled out a long envelope. It was from the Director of Research and Development.

'Whatever's he writing to us about?' asked Sister Mary Clare, who was laying the cutlery out on the table.

'Just a minute, stop what you're doing, it's quite exciting . . . I'll read it aloud to you. Oh yes, there's this press cutting enclosed too. It's about our building project.' Waving the *Press and Journal* cutting at her I began to read the accompanying letter.

In brief, the Director of the Research and Development Department said that he was interested in our building project, and wondered if I had ever thought of Brough Lodge as an alternative. He brought his letter to a close by inviting us to meet him and discuss it further, if we were interested.

We looked at each other across the room somewhat amazed. 'Not Brough Lodge again,' I groaned. 'Just when I thought I'd got it out of my system.'

'I think that we should go and talk to him all the same,' retorted my irrepressible Sister. 'I know that we aren't interested in it as a suitable home for us, yet it would make a wonderful Retreat House.'

'Yes, I'm afraid you're right,' I replied, thinking particularly of two of our Caim members, Keith and Eunice. Keith was a priest, and along with his wife Eunice, was particularly drawn towards the idea of retreat work. Not only that, but they had been having, for several months, some disquieting thoughts that they might be being called north.

On a cold December day just before Christmas we set off for Lerwick, having arranged that when we had finished our shopping we would go along to the Research and Development Department offices for our appointment which we were expecting to be in the form of a cosy chat.

'Be careful,' Sister Mary Clare warned me as we stepped out of the car in the glow of the street lights. 'It's very icy.'

Throwing a scarf around my neck I clambered out into the sharp evening air and we slithered over to the entrance of the building. It was warm inside and since there was no one at the reception desk we sat down thankfully on the upright chairs provided and waited, glad to get off our feet after trailing round with heavy shopping. Our reprieve was not for long though, for almost as soon as we had made ourselves comfortable, in stamped two men in overcoats, carrying briefcases. They dropped down on the two remaining seats and smiled across at us.

'I think that we're all heading for the same meeting,' said the older man. 'We're from the Planning Office.'

'Meeting!' we chorused. 'We're only expecting an informal little talk.'

At this moment a lady came in and beckoned us through into the bowels of the department. 'Do come this way . . yes, just through here. Now, if you would take a seat around this table . . . Mr Burgess will be with you shortly.' He entered as the lady left the room, his arm outstretched to welcome us, and without more ado we seated ourselves at the large table and began the most exciting meeting that we had ever attended, one which could turn out to have a long-term effect on the work of our community. The immediate and exciting outcome for us was that we were invited to apply to the Research and Development Department for a substantial grant towards our two visitors' chalets and our craft workshop.

Christmas came around again in all its glory, and this year Sister Mary Clare wondered if it might not be a good idea to do something slightly different. 'Instead of having the Fetlar bairns to their usual children's service and then after tea traipsing around the isle carol singing with them, why don't we put out an invitation to the whole island, to a candlelit service? We could invite mothers and fathers, grannies and grandpas and aunts and uncles too, as well as the children and hold it in the byre/chapel . . . and wouldn't it be nice if we could acquire a Shetland pony, and what about bringing in Samantha the sheep . . . We could still do it as you always have, as a preparation for Christmas . . .'

Our large byre/chapel was full, and how lovely it looked with the babe, a life-sized doll, lying in a real manger and spotlighted as a focal point in the flickering light. During the service of carols and lessons the children and I processed to the cattle stall with candles. There we stood around the babe to sing their special carol, 'Away in a manger'. Because our congregation were shy, each member of the community read a lesson. Sister Mary Clare spoke of the shepherds and of how much we in our island life can relate to those humble, privileged men. Rosemary recited most beautifully Christina Rossetti's 'In the bleak mid-winter', bringing out a whole new dimension to the carol so often sung. Rose said the prayer for the day and Frances, between all this, accompanied us on the little electronic organ. Later she led the bairns in the ringing of handbells, which she had taught them up at the school. In fact they rang the service to a glorious end with 'Good King Wenceslas'. We did not, I must add, bring in Samantha or a pony, though Sister Mary Clare is still working on it!

Afterwards, jubilant and happy we and all our friends squashed into the tiny but room in The Ness to sup hot cups of tea and devour a quantity of mince pies.

The tiny but room is now festooned in its Christmas apparel. Bedecked with hundreds of cards hung from the beams, along with two large bunches of balloons which one has to duck under and a jolly table decoration made by Sister Mary Clare, it looks most welcoming. The electric fire, set back into the fireplace, is aglow and, also tucked into the fireplace, stands the Christmas tree – not the traditional fir, but a small branch pruned from one of the elder bushes out in the garden. One of our kind friends from Exeter always sends us a few Christmas decorations as part of her Christmas gift. So the little tree becomes more resplendent with each year that passes. In the passage-room, just through the door by which I'm standing, is a spare bed which, at this moment, is spread with parcels yet to be opened.

It's Christmas Eve, and as usual I have chosen as my allotted task on this day, to decorate the but room. Sister Mary Clare is in the chapel, arranging the flowers which amazingly, we've managed to buy from Lerwick. Frances is renewing the chapel candles and Rosemary, who is also in the byre/chapel, is attaching a model of an ox and an ass's head, which she made long ago, to the door of the manger stall.

There are just a few more cards to hang up, and as I collect them from the passage-room bed, I can't help having a sneaky feel at a particularly interesting-looking parcel! No, I haven't a clue what it is and, knowing that the rest of the family won't approve of me tweaking it, I return to the but room with the cards.

Always, I sense the presence of many people with us in spirit during this lovely season and thank God for the gift of Himself in all of them. Also, I thank Him for the manifestation of Himself in all things, in our lives in their simplicity and in all that we do, whether it's lighting the peat fire in the ben room next door, washing the dishes, writing letters, working with our hands, ministering to the needs of those whom He sends here or singing His praises. Yes, and also in the showing of His love in all our little animal friends, in the beauty of the island, in the land and sea and in the elements. Above all, I thank him for His love in His Son Jesus Christ, who so perfectly showed us the way, the truth and the life of love.

During my early life in religion I thought that many of these things had to be denied in the attainment of perfection. This included marriage, the wonderment of beauty in creation and the loving of a little creature like a cat or dog or tiny bird. So, instead of adoring God, as I longed to do, in and through the natural world which He'd spread around us, I felt that one of the greatest priorities of life was denial. It was later that I rebelled against this denial in the realisation that all these things are holy, in that God's own loveliness shines from them. For we are servants and stewards entrusted with a precious mystery. A mystery which I look forward to an even greater revelation of, in heaven.

In my chrysalis stage of growing and understanding I tried to write poetry. I knew nothing about it, yet something in me forced itself in this way to be free. It was love, for love is freedom and cannot exist imprisoned in our bodies, minds or hearts.

With apologies for its inadequate fumblings and roughness of style I include this so-called sonnet which I've left standing as it was written long ago, like a child's first scrawlings at school.

> Why try, O fickle beauty, why, to woo
> Me with thy graces? Or to charm my ear
> Or eye, or by some haunting word pierce through
> My soul, or wrapped in nature's garb endear?
> For lo, no captivating spell shall lure
> Me falsely thus to love thee. I must die . . .
> And in abandonment of self, endure
> My cross. That through death's degradation, I
> Might rise and risen cry . . . 'At last, Lord, bless.'
> . . . Ah yes . . . It is Himself I see, yet He
> Just sighs and says, 'Love lies in loveliness.'
> . . . O now, sweet beauty, I who cast thee down
> Will love thee truly, thou, whom Love doth crown.

15 *Freedom's Pinions*

Since Rosemary arrived to live at Lower Ness, it has been our custom to share our Sunday lunch at her house. On 20th January 1991 we all gathered together around her large kitchen table and as always had a superb meal. After lunch she generally gives us a cup of tea or coffee in the ben room, and sometimes in the happy daze of a Sunday afternoon we stay on to chat or listen to music. On this particular Sunday I excused myself immediately after the meal since I had several letters to get into the post. It was a raw day, and as I shut her door and made my way through the front garden I suddenly caught sight of Samantha. Samantha is Rosemary's yowe, who had been brought up by us as a kiddy lamb a few years previously. Something about her made me call her name across the field. To this she responded at once and was soon nuzzling my hand through the garden fence. She had grown into a lovely sheep though was not, I noticed, looking in peak condition at that moment. Sheep nuts were in the forefront of her mind I was sure, so leaning over the fence I pacified her with a pat on the head. As I did so I heard a whimpering, pathetic bleat. Peering further over the fence I saw, incredulously, a tiny lamb leaning on four unsteady legs against her rump and still covered in afterbirth. 'But this is January, isn't it?' I asked myself, 'and Shetland lambing doesn't begin until the middle of May at the earliest . . . Just a minute though, there was a moorit ram, who became quite a good friend of ours and who very tiresomely would jump fences. We spent much time at one stage moving him back to the paddock where he belonged . . . Well I never, good old Samantha – a lamb on the Eve of St Agnes!' Quickly I turned tail and dashed back to the house. 'Come at once,' I yelled. 'Samantha's got a lamb.'

'Trust old Samantha,' said Rosemary, collecting up a handful of nuts for her. 'Come on, girl, follow me.'

Picking up the wet little lamb I followed her too, and Sister Mary Clare, Frances and Rose all went ahead to open the appropriate gates and prepare one of the cattle stalls in the back of the byre/chapel for its new residents. Half an hour later, Samantha and her baby were bedded down on a comfortable mound of soft hay, whilst we leaned drooling over the door.

'I know – as it's your jubilee year, Sister Agnes,' said Rosemary turning towards me, 'let's call the little one Jubilee.'

So Jubilee she was named and now, exactly a year later to the day, as I write this chapter, she is munching grass outside my window, along with her mother with whom she has stayed great friends. She is a beautiful young ewe and I know that Sister Mary Clare has a beady eye on her fleece for spinning.

Jubilee's advent was the first of about two dozen early lambs, so the next few months were busy for us, especially for Sister Mary Clare acting as chief sheperdess. Our friends Andrew and Sheila, to whom the flock belongs, run the Harbour Trust farm on the Shetland Mainland and only come out to Fetlar at intervals. Meanwhile we try to keep an eye on things for them. It seems a good way of repaying them for all the kindness they have shown to us.

On this occasion, as the lambs were coming unexpectedly early, the sheep needed daily feeding. This meant giving them a bale of hay and a bag of sheep nuts every morning after our

Office of Terce. Sister Mary Clare and I tried to do the job together since there was invariably a stampede when we were seen approaching the building where the hay was stored. Without support, one person alone could easily get mobbed, as indeed had happened on one of the days when I was busy with another job. Hearing the noise, I had glanced through a window to see Sister Mary Clare astride a huge ewe, and closed in by what looked like a hundred other ravenous beasties all bleating their throats sore for more food. Precariously balanced, she could only wave the remains of a decimated bag of sheep nuts and cry for help.

Despite the mud, chilblains from the cold winter blasts, and the hard toil of such work, we thoroughly enjoyed this new aspect of our lifestyle. In a way, it very much helped balance it in as much as the outdoor work complemented the increasing amount of office work we were having to work at with regard to the building project. Also, as we had the honour of being recognised officially as a community, this meant that we were automatically recognised as a charity. This brought with it a whole series of unwanted complications. First of all it meant that we had to work at a mound of book work that previously we had never bothered with. For however small an amount of money that now came in, whether as a donation or as earned income, it had to be recorded. Also an account had to be kept for the Inland Revenue of every penny that went out. Also, as grants were awarded to us, we were asked to produce cash flow charts of how we expected to make good with what had been entrusted to us. In other words, we had to show how the craft workshop and the two visitors' chalets were going to cover all their expenses and make a substantial profit at the end of the day. We had no idea of course, when we started out, of all this extra involvement and suddenly felt inescapably hemmed in by bureaucracy. Often I feel like throwing all our paperwork over the banks into the sea. Irresponsible perhaps, though we felt then and indeed feel still, like spiders entangled in a web of legislation, who are constantly asking themselves where their ideals of simplicity and freedom have gone.

As well as all this, Sister Mary Clare was negotiating to take on the Stakkafletts council house for the use of our summer visitors, whilst I, on my side of things, battled to keep up with the ever-increasing number of letters that poured in. Yes, trying to live the religious life within its ordered framework as we wished to live it was becoming difficult for the two of us at the centre of the community. On top of our day-by-day responsibilities, the feeding of two hundred ewes, scouring the croft for newborn lambs and bottle-feeding some of them, was more than we could cope with. Sometimes we had as many as five yowes and their youngsters at a time. Something, we realised, had to be done about the pace of our lives. Though what, was the question.

However, despite our busyness there were lots of joys and two of them were Foula and Ramling. Foula was a much later lamb who had been abandoned by her mother and whom we first saw following Sheila around in a pathetic-lost-lambish sort of way. Sheila, who had come up to Fetlar for a fortnight during the official lambing season, had found this wee mite along with its dead twin. The mother sheep had had no milk and certainly no interest in her offspring. So when the time came for Sheila to leave, she handed Foula into Sister Mary Clare's tender care. 'If you can pull her through you can keep her . . . that's of course if you want her,' Sheila generously offered.

Foula was cossetted, fed every few hours, talked to and loved until gradually she began to show real signs of life and growth. She was even put into a cat basket and taken off to Da Gaets with us for a week, when we needed to go to Lerwick on all sorts of errands. She rapidly thrived and enjoys life to the full along wih her inseparable pal Ramling.

Our friend Kenny had discovered Ramling in much the same state as Foula had been. Knowing that he was one of Andrew and Sheila's flock he kindly brought him down from the hill and tethered him outside his croft house with two other caddies of his own. After a week or two, Kenny's lambs were moved on and Ramling, awaiting Andrew and Sheila's next visit to Fetlar, was so lonely without them that he bleated ceaselessly and almost drove Kenny and his wife Mimie mad.

It was at that stage that the little fellow was delivered to us and instantly took a liking to Foula. This was so obvious, that we decided almost at once that we must keep him, though we realised of course that we would need to get him 'seen to'. Some of our crofting friends thought that we were behaving in an extremely 'English' manner, despite the fact that we strengthened our argument by reminding them what a beautiful nut-brown fleece he would give us each year.

The big caravan is a lovely bolt-hole to escape to when it's not occupied by visitors. I'm sitting in it now and enjoying a little recreational time with a book. Many of our friends have sent books as gifts over the years, so that now, along with the largesse of about a hundred which Rosemary originally gave me from her own library when I first came to Fetlar, we have a good selection. These include old and modern, fiction and non-fiction, and of course spiritual and secular. What I'm reading at the moment is the latest riveting novel about the medieval detective monk Brother Cadfael, which I've borrowed from the travelling library.

The library van comes to Fetlar once every three weeks and our friend Donald the librarian knows each of our tastes and triumphantly produced this new Brother Cadfael for me, last time he was here.

Yes, our lifestyle here allows for reading and we each always have two books on hand and if we wish, a third. The first two are the Bible and a theological or spiritual book of some sort, and the third can be any form of light reading. All help to succour us in our remote location, and some assist us to see different slants on life, as does the small portable television that we've recently been given by Alma and Dennis. Also, our spiritual and theological reading helps tremendously to keep us abreast with new thought and growth in the Church.

One of the lovely things which many of the visitors whom we've entertained here come for, is to find time to read. This cosy caravan sitting-room, with its large window looking out to sea, has been a place in which many have found both inspiration and a new direction to their lives. Looking out through the window now, I'm enjoying the beauty of our headland, plus the added pleasure of seeing our new building, Tigh Sith, which means House of Peace and which has blended so beautifully into the landscape. I can also enjoy the thought that within that building's two little chalet units, which are so much better protected than this caravan, many other souls will be led along new paths in their quest for truth. All of which, to my mind, lead to the attainment of that great meaning of life – Love.

My watch tells me that it's time to feed the animals, which I've promised to do for Sister Mary Clare today as she's out shopping on Yell. Already, Foula and Ramling are looking pleadingly in through the window, and the cats and Tildy have been rampaging for at least ten minutes in their efforts to convey to me that it's time for their tea. Last and not least, the little goat, Iona, is bleating. Ah well, I must put down Brother Cadfael, and slip a marker into the place that I've reached, with the hopes of returning to it perhaps, who knows, tomorrow.

Now, having stepped out through the door into the blinding sunlight I'm immediately buffeted by two warm, woolly bodies and shown the way back to the house by a convoy of cats with a wiggly dog at their rear. As I trip between my charges I'm aware, once again, of a song in the air, a song of love which captures the essence of truth, wherever and however we may look for it.

> *The nearest way to God*
> *Leads through love's open door*
> *The path of knowledge is*
> *Too slow for evermore.*[1]

16 Widening Circles

At last, with the lambing behind us, old friends and new began again to arrive for retreat times and quiet holidays. Simon, a scientist, and his delightful wife Joan, were two of the first to come. Simon had introduced himself to me some years ago whilst he and Joan were having a few days' holiday on the Fetlar camping site. Actually, I had received a letter from him written a week earlier and was, by the time he arrived, aware of a great problem that he was thrashing around in his mind, trying to solve. We talked deeply and I remember thinking what a nice person he was. On the strength of our meeting we became good friends and to our joy, almost every year since, Simon and Joan have returned to the Isles. Mostly they have come in their motor-home, and whilst on Fetlar have usually helped with an assortment of jobs. Simon is wont now to ring up before they leave home and ask what kind of hat we would like him to wear. He is an exceptionally good electrician, so electrical repairs are often at the top of our 'hat' list.

This year, 1991, instead of coming during the summer months they arrived in the spring, bearing in their arms a most wonderful gift for my Silver Jubilee of making vows. It was a word processor, especially welcome since I was in the process of signing a contract to write this sequel to *A Tide that Sings*. They knew that I had written my first book in longhand and would soon be starting the next, and that such a gift would make life easier. We were all completely nonplussed by such generosity – and what transformation it has made to our lives, especially to mine.

Another slight transformation, or should I say inroad into our lives at this time was that we were given a monetary gift that the community thought I ought to spend on driving lessons. This I did, though it meant the tremendous effort of travelling to Lerwick once a week. However, it was great fun in as much as our friend Aileen, who lives on Fetlar, bravely offered to come along too and give me moral support. So it worked out that Aileen had her lesson at eleven o'clock and I, with the same instructor, at twelve. Afterwards, we would meet for a cheap lunch somewhere before coming home.

The Silver Jubilee of my Simple Vows fell on 1st March 1991. Since the community wanted to make an occasion of it by inviting several close friends and Caim members from the far south, we decided that the date for the celebration should be moved. March was an attrocious month, weather-wise, to expect folk either to travel up or stay in Shetland, so instead, 1st July was chosen.

Between the visit of Simon and Joan and the Silver Jubilee celebrations, time and energy were put into the filling up of forms, the visiting of this department and that of the Shetland Islands Council and of various individuals, as well as producing possible cash flow charts and such other disagreeable things. Sister Mary Clare took the brunt of all this and did so efficiently, despite not relishing the work. In fact she was so good at it, that just before the Jubilee we received the unbelievable news that we had been allocated thirty-eight thousand pounds towards the project from the Shetland Islands Council Research and Development Department. This was not, they stipulated, towards our home and chapel. 'We're not interested in that phase,' they wrote, 'but only in the two visitors' units and the craft workshop.' Even more astonishingly, we were told by our new friend Mandy (who works for the department and who had presented our application to the Council) that the grant which we were being given had to go hand-in-hand with another grant from a Trust known as Shetland Enterprise. After more meetings and more filling in of forms the SE grant was also given us – a specifically allocated amount of twenty-five thousand pounds to be spent on equipping the building.

Reeling from shock we started the ball rolling with regard to the erection of the visitors' units and the craft workshop. Because we had received the grants we were obliged, of course, to plough all the money we had previously raised for the house and chapel into this first phase. Our hope is that we won't have to wait too many decades to recover it in order to build our home. We have, however, been promised a sum of fifteen thousand pounds from the Shetland Churches' Trust towards the chapel – when that day comes.

Muddled in with all this project work, invitations were sent out and preparations made for the Jubilee. What a relief it was that we were to have Number One Stakkafletts in which to accommodate some of our guests. However, there was only one problem. As we had decided to hold on to Da Gaets we had no spare furniture. 'Ah well,' we thought, 'we shall have to jump that hurdle when we come to it.' Top of our priorities at that particular moment, having been given the key to the house, was to decorate it.

All five of us turned to with buckets and mops. Then Rosemary, Rose and Sister Mary Clare emulsioned walls, Frances screwed up curtain rails, and I jigsawed oddments of carpet to the stairs. We even had Frances' brother and his wife, who were staying with her that week, wiping down the kitchen walls and checking out the plumbing and electricity. By the time we had finished it was sparkling and we still had a whole month in which to decide how to furnish it.

Days sped past into June, when soon our visitors would be arriving. Keith and Eunice were to be among them, along with their daughter Emily, and we had decided that they should be the family to stay in Number One. Urgently now, we scanned the *Shetland Times* for secondhand bits and pieces of furniture; in this way we managed to find one bed, a Baby Belling cooker and an electric sweeper.

Sister Mary Clare needed a final shopping expedition to Lerwick before the celebration. She promised to make a few enquiries with regard to our furniture problem, otherwise we would have to transport furniture temporarily from Da Gaets. On this grey day, when she set out, what a surprise it was to her to meet up with our friend Liz, whose ordination we had attended before Sister Mary Clare joined me. Liz was, at this point, excitedly making arrangements for another great event in her life. She, a widow, was about to marry Stewart, a widower, and since they were amalgamating their homes they had masses of furniture to get rid of quickly. Everyone has problems!

'Hi,' said Liz. 'What a dreadful day, though it's good to see you.'

'And good to see you, Liz. How are all your arrangements coming on for the wedding?'

'Frustratingly slow,' she grimaced. 'Actually, I'm just on my way to the Social Services office to see if they can get rid of some furniture for me. You should see my house. It's like a bomb site with all the packing up that's going on. If only I could get rid of the stuff we don't need . . .'

Sister Mary Clare's jaw dropped . . . later that day, before she had even arrived home, I had a telephone call from Liz.

'Would you really like our old bits and pieces?' she asked. 'I'd rather you had them than anyone.'

'Thank you, thank you, Liz. I can't tell you what an answer to prayer this is.'

'Oh, don't thank me. You're doing us a favour, Sister Agnes, by having it.'

Excitedly we then made our arrangements to have the furniture transported to Fetlar.

How adequately – and beautifully – Liz's cupboards, chairs, tables, bookcases and beds furnished the house. How thrilled we were that not only was it ready in time for our Jubilee guests, but also for our diocesan Chancellor friend from Ellon, who had asked to come and stay for a few days. He, who was the first of many to use and appreciate the house, has written the Foreword to this book.

Soon, guests began to arrive for 1st July, including my father's sister, Aunty Edna, and her friend Betty, who are both Caim members. What a tremendous pleasure it was to have my family represented in Aunty Edna, since neither Carole, my sister, nor my stepmother, were able to come. Aunty Edna and Betty stayed at Lower Ness with Rosemary; Joan, a Caim member from Edinburgh, stayed with Frances and Rose; Sybil, still our newest Caim member, stayed with Mimie. Then Di, who has camped in Lower Ness garden each summer with her husband and family, and who is also a Caim member, camped again. Of course Eunice and Keith were at Number One and thrilled to be there. Though even greater was their delight when we asked them if they would put the Bishop up for the night. Bishop Frederick was with us to preach at one of the two Jubilee services. He, of course, had helped us with the rent for Number One and was delighted with what he saw.

One of the most memorable things about our Jubilee celebration was the spirit of joy that permeated the week. Rather wonderfully, it was upon this subject that our friend and Guardian, the Bishop, preached. In this way our Service of Thanksgiving on the 30th June was made an especially moving and happy one.

The byre/chapel was full to overflowing with ourselves, our guests, and our island friends who were not only from Fetlar but from all over Shetland. They included a group of singers who had offered their time and talent for the day, and a group of friends from St Colman's church on Yell.

Lastly, there was with us an ITV production team. I had battled fiercely against having them, though finally agreed because they were such a nice crew, caused no problems, nor in any way spoilt the atmosphere of the service. With them came our good friend Ted Harrison. Ted, whom some may remember as the Religious Affairs Correspondent for BBC Radio Four, brought along his wife Helen, a professional singer, who had offered to sing an aria from Handel's Messiah at our Eucharist on 1st July. This was a great joy. Another joy was that they brought with them a giant box of white lilies and chrysanthemums. This was a surprise for me, and indeed I could never have imagined such a gift or with what splendour the byre/chapel would be decorated.

At the end of the Service of Thanksgiving we had a procession from the byre/chapel, which is dedicated to the Holy Cross, down to the site of the new chapel out on the headland. The new site, at this stage, was only partly marked out in lime.

Bishop Frederick wearing mitre and vestments, headed the procession behind Father Keith, who carried the processional cross. Actually, we had wondered what on earth we were going to do about a processional cross since we did not have one. However, two days before we needed it, there arrived a lovely hamper of goodies from Exeter, and wrapped carefully on the top, as a gift to me for my Jubilee was – an Assisi Cross! That particular cross is painted in the most beautiful blues, reds, blacks, white and pinks, and amazingly, was just the size of the cross that we needed. So, 'nothing venture nothing win', I attached it to a long pole of wood and then passed it on to Rosemary, who sandpapered the pole and then painted it a brilliant red. It was magnificent, especially when, to add a finishing touch, she tied around it a white bow of ribbon. However, she confessed later, that as Father Keith clasped it to his bosom, against his pristine white alb, she nervously wondered if it were in fact quite dry!

For our processional hymn we sang 'Lift high the Cross', a perfect choice which took us all the way to the piece of ground where our new buildings were to be erected. Once there, the Bishop blessed the site, and immediately after, to the immense surprise of everyone including myself, a peal of bells rang out over and over again. It was Frances, bless her, who had secretly formed a group of handbell ringers from amongst our guests and had placed them on the mound above us all. They rang this memorable occasion to an end most beautifully.

We heard later, that from a distance, some bird watchers had witnessed the whole proceedings through their binoculars. The proceedings, of course, included the television cameras so no wonder that they thought some great historical film was being made. With the Bishop striding ahead, crook in hand, his robes streaming in the wind and looking for all the world like St Columba himself, we could imagine how easily they could have been mistaken.

After tea in the island hall and after the cutting of the cake and our farewells to those who had the ferry to catch we walked back to The Ness and all, in Sister Mary Clare's words, 'collopsed!'

Later, there was a grand barbecue on The Ness beach for everyone who wished. This was a new experience for some of us, including our tribe of animals who gambolled around, sharing in the fun.

This unforgettable occasion owed much to many people who made it such a success. To Rosemary, with her loving, stalwart and cheerful encouragement – constant throughout the years. To Sister Mary Clare, my 'Personal Pedestal Polisher', who keeps me down to size when others would do otherwise, and shows such loyalty and love, and who put an enormous amount of work into organising the celebration. To Frances, who distils quiet wholeheartedness among us as a group, and gave exuberant music lessons to community and visitors alike – what fun our choir practices in the big caravan were! To Rose, who oversaw all the catering arrangements for this event – a mammoth task – and who bestows a gentle healing touch upon everyone.

All our Caim members, too, gave their prayerful and practical support, especially those who were actually with us at the Jubilee, and not only shared in all our work and preparations for it but also shared, so wholeheartedly, in our worship and fun times too. We thank God, that in their meeting together they formed an especially strong bond – one which is still, almost tangibly, felt in their encirclement around us.

Lastly, I am most thankful to Bishop Frederick for accepting me into his Diocese of Aberdeen and Orkney in 1984 and thus making our rejoicing at this time possible. Also, that he so wisely placed my own and later SOLI's spiritual welfare in the hands of Father Lewis our dear friend and adviser.

The Jubilee celebrations over, we tried to get back to something that savoured of normality and found it well-night impossible. Visitors came and went, and in due course the building contractor, along with our engineer, arrived to finish marking out the site before work commenced the following week. Alas, the contractor declared that the higher level, upon which we were expecting to build the visitors' units, was too small, too rocky for drains to be put in easily and would need extortionately expensive foundations, as much of that area is hard-core. He suggested, in short, that we needed to go back to the drawing board. This was a great blow to us as we were short on time. Also, we did not want the construction period to run too far into the autumn, when in Shetland daylight becomes short and the weather rough.

As quickly as possible, Peter and Bryan drew up another

plan which, instead of allowing for the visitors' units to be built up on the mound, tacked them on to the end of the craft workshop, under the same roof, down below. Again, plans were presented for Building Warrant and patiently we waited.

Not surprisingly it was September before the foundations were started and the kit arrived, after which we had an average of five or six workmen to feed for many weeks. The brickies came first, and then the joiners, the brickies again, and again the joiners. After which came the plumbers, electricians and finally the decorators. How thankful we were, yet again, for the Stakkafletts house in which to accommodate them. For of course, living on an island means that we invariably have to house workmen who can only get home at weekends.

With the building schedule starting later than planned we ran into the complication of Sister Mary Clare, our chief cook, having to be away when we most desperately needed her. I was daunted by the thought of having to feed five or six hungry workmen each day – at that time, without a shop in the island, this was no mean feat. However, Rosemary, Frances and a kindly visitor who was staying, were a tremendous help and on the whole the three weeks that Sister Mary Clare was away, went remarkably smoothly. Her absence was all wonderfully worthwhile in the end, too, since she was representing us in presenting our building project to the Diocesan Synod. The outcome of this presentation won us another gift of eight thousand pounds.

The day on which I drove Sister Mary Clare to the south of the Shetland Mainland to catch her flight to Aberdeen was the day the joiners arrived to start on the actual erection of the kit. What an amazing sight it was to arrive home late that night and see, with the aid of a torch, that where there had been only a rocky field there now stood what looked like a large house. The whole structure was upright and already boarded, with a skeleton roof. How sorry we were that Sister Mary Clare had missed this excitement and was to miss many others as she had to go on down to Devon to visit her mother. What a joy it was for us all when she returned and what a lot we had to show her.

Eventually we said goodbye to the building constructors and settled our thoughts towards the winter. I now had to work on the writing of this book, for my deadline was March and there was the busyness of Christmas in between.

As I shuffle along a row of carrots, thinning them out in a mechanical sort of way, I enjoy the warmth of the sun on my back. With such a job there's plenty of time to think, and today my thoughts return to another garden in Devon sixteen years ago, where I was possibly doing the same thing.

Rosemary was there too, in the same garden, and I remember exactly what she was doing. She was emptying a barrow load of weeds. She'd paused on the garden path close at hand and mopped her brow, for it was hot in the Devon sunshine. Pushing her handkerchief away she'd asked quietly, 'Are we courageous enough to pray, "Come Holy Ghost"? Seconds passed . . . only the sound of birdsong filled the air, for I could not answer at once. After a moment she continued. 'Sister Agnes, if we pray that prayer, we must expect anything . . .'

'Yes, Rosemary,' I'd said, 'let's pray it, and let's pray it now . . .'

Come, Holy Ghost, our souls inspire,
And lighten with celestial fire;
Thou the anointing Spirit art,
Who dost Thy sevenfold gifts impart:

Thy blessed unction from above
Is comfort, life, and fire of love;
Enable with perpetual light
The dullness of our blinded sight:

Anoint and cheer our soiled face
With the abundance of Thy grace:
Keep far our foes, keep peace at home;
Where Thou art guide no ill can come.

Teach us to know the Father, Son,
And Thee, of Both, to be but One;
That through the ages all along
This may be our endless song,

> *Praise to thy eternal merit,*
> *Father, Son, and Holy Spirit.*[1]

Rosemary had looked across at me as she lifted the handles of her
wheelbarrow. 'Yes, William Temple said something like this: ''He
who prays in the power of the Holy Spirit, must mind what he is
about . . .'''

17 A Migrant

'Sister Mary Clare, could you answer the phone?'

In the kitchen with my arms in a bowl of soapy suds, I listened hard to see if I could catch who it might be at the other end of the line.

'Yes, . . . yes . . . Oh no! . . . I am sorry. Are you still at the airport? Can you . . . Mmm, I understood. Can you find lodgings for the night? . . . Good . . .'

Deducing that it was our new friend Pat, who was on her way from New Zealand, and that she was not likely to be arriving the next day as planned, I continued with the washing-up. A few moments later, Sister Mary Clare came into the kitchen, lit a ring on the gas stove and put on the kettle. Taking up a tea-towel she wiped a couple of mugs. 'That was Pat,' she said. She opened the cupboard door and reached into it for the coffee jar. 'Let's have a cup of coffee, then I can tell you all about Pat's adventures.'

A moment or so later we were sitting in front of the ben room fire which was aglow with peats. As the firelight danced across the walls we realised that soon, although we had only just had lunch, we must light the lamps and a candle or two. Outside the wind was howling; it had been howling for days now and had, only the night before, thrown over on to its side the Greenbank caravan which had been Rose's, and which she had recently passed on to Frances. It had been well anchored with ropes and walled in, but even so had not withstood the force of the gale. 'Ah well,' Frances had commented philosophically, 'at least no one was in it. It doesn't look too badly damaged, and now I'll be able to paint its underneaths!' The gales had also done damage to a hydro-electricity cable on Yell which, if serious, meant that we could be without power for days. This, of course, is all part of the winter pattern.

I put a large spoonful of sugar in my coffee and I stirred it around. 'Well, what's happened to Pat?'

'She's stuck in Aberdeen for the night. Her plane's been grounded due to weather conditions.'

This news did not surprise us. Neither did it surprise us when a few days later Pat told us that, having taken her forty-eight hours to travel between her home in New Zealand and Aberdeen, it had then taken her five days to reach Fetlar. Consequently she had had to spend several extra nights en route in Aberdeen, Orkney and Lerwick. Poor Pat, much of her hard-earned money had needed to be spent on telephone calls and boarding houses, so that by the time she arrived, there was little left. This kind of saga is why we advise people not to visit us during the winter months. With Pat it was a slightly different matter, for being a school teacher, she had arranged her visit to coincide with her New Zealand school's summer holidays.

Pat, in Christchurch, had heard about the kind of life that I lived on Fetlar through some friends who had visited me three years previously. She had read an article in a Shetland/New Zealand magazine about their visit and had started to write to me herself. It was during our correspondence that she began to feel the stirrings of a real call to Fetlar. As always in such a case, I suggested that she give herself a year to think quietly about it. This she agreed to do and found herself another post as head teacher of a small school in a rural area where she could better experience living alone. Having struggled to bring up a family of five children almost single-handed, being solitary was a lifestyle unknown to her. Yet by the end of her year she was still as adamant in her decision. Almost enough money had been set aside for her fare, and more importantly and wonderfully, she had splendid backing from her now grown-up children. So her arrangements were made to come to Europe for a short holiday to see how we all felt.

It was during our final exchange of letters with Pat regarding her visit that she told me excitedly of a recent discovery that her mother, whom she had never known, had come from Shetland, from a place called Walls. Writing back, equally thrilled, I told her that our little hermitage cottage was only five or six miles over the hill from Walls. This is, of course, no distance in Shetland where we can travel fifty miles or more to shop without turning a hair.

We had awaited Pat's coming with anticipation, and were not disappointed when she arrived. She is large, witful, has a lovely sense of humour and an abundance of common sense. We liked her immediately and the only question in our minds was that if we accepted her we would be taking another person over fifty. However, who are we to say? I am sure that the Holy Spirit does not take age into account.

Pat was to be with us over Christmas, along with a very much younger person named Kerry, who had asked to come in order to have some emergency convalescence with us as she was recuperating after a long stay in hospital. Kerry, from Aberdeen, is a lovely girl in her early twenties. Having her to stay brought back a long-forgotten memory of how I, in my teens, had decided with no doubts at all, that when I was married, my first daughter would be called Kerry.

We put our new friends each into one of the chalet units, having had all the furniture from the Stakkafletts council house transferred down to the new building. Our agreement with the housing department had been that we should have the use of the house for as long as no one needed it as a home. This need had eventually arisen, and grateful for the privilege of having used it, we handed back the key. We now had our own units for visitors and had spent most of the week before Pat and Kerry arrived getting them ready. At the same time we battled again with Christmas mail, and I with my manuscript. Rosemary polished furniture and hunted around her own home for bits and pieces that were still needed, such as a milk jug or a fruit bowl, or enough knives and forks. Sister Mary Clare sat at the sewing machine in the craft workshop and turned up the hems of curtains whilst Frances dotted around with a step ladder putting up curtain rails and the curtains themselves. I, with a handful of screws and a bit and a brace, fixed up hooks and hangers, toilet roll holders and a couple of mirrors. Unbelievably, we were ready by the time our guests arrived. So these two lovely people were the first guests to stay there, which was for the period over Christmas and the New Year.

Christmastide was spent mostly by a large fire in the ben room at The Ness. The ben room had also, over the past year, doubled as my bedroom – that is, since I had bullied Sister Mary Clare into having the neuk upstairs. However, during the times when I am not sleeping in it, and with my bed covered to look like a couch, it makes a cosy room in which to sit.

Over Christmas week we try to be as free as possible and do only necessary chores. Our custom has become that each household takes it in turn to provide the main mid-day meal during the three Holy Days. This year, Sister Mary Clare and I provided the suppers too, which were very light and eaten around the hearth.

Due to the gales, which meant many days without electricity, most of the festival was spent by candlelight, in the way it had started in the byre/chapel. As in the previous year, we invited our local friends to join us on Christmas Eve for a service of carols and lessons, ending with a joyous peal of bells. On this occasion we did not pile into The Ness afterwards for refreshments. Instead, with a sprinkling of snow on our boots, we trooped down to Tigh Sith.

Later that same evening, long after our island friends had departed, we, the community, and our two guests, met together in the byre/chapel, this time to participate in the lovely service which ends with the making of our communions at midnight in the oratory. There was the usual procession out of doors from the chapel to the oratory, at which we usually carried a lighted candle. This is prone to blow out as we step through the byre/chapel door into the wind, so this time we tried to defeat the elements by each clutching what turned out to be a totally unsatisfactory battery candle – so much for modern technology.

Before we knew where we were it was New Year's Eve, the electricity had been resumed and Pat and Kerry had persuaded us to see the New Year in with them down in the craft workshop. At least that was the idea, although Rosemary and Frances had both definitely decided that neither of them could stay up so late. However, as midnight drew nearer, the wind became fiercer and Sister Mary Clare and I both seriously wondered if we were wise to venture out of doors to Tigh Sith.

'They'll be terribly disappointed if we don't show up, and there is no way that we can get a message to them,' I said. 'Look, I'll pop outside the back door and see just how bad it is.' A few moments later I returned. 'If we wrap up well in something waterproof against the rain which is lashing down, and if we hang tightly on to each other, I think we'll make it. Are you game?'

Within five minutes we were bundled up against the weather and with torches in our hands we set off. To start with we seemed to take more steps backwards than forwards.

'Let's bend our bodies almost double.' shouted Sister Mary Clare above the roar of the gale, and fold them into the wind.' We did this and it made an amazing difference, though we did not realise at the time just how foolish we were. Breathless, we reached the workshop door and fell over the threshold where shrieks of delight greeted us.

'Hurrah, hurrah!' chorused two very surprised voices from within. 'Hurrah, well done . . . you've made it. We gave you up long ago . . . Do come in, take off your wet things and sit down.' The workshop looked festive and welcoming with a few coloured candles flickering here and there. A couple of electric lights were switched on, though were blinking ominously.

Actually, it had taken us such a long time to come down the right of way, that by the time we arrived midnight had ticked away by about five minutes, so wishing each other a happy New Year we sat down to drink each other's health in a concoction specially prepared for us by Kerry, our Scot. It was hot and delicious and just what we needed. Whilst sipping it against the noisy background of the battering wind, we nostalgically remembered the past year and thought hopefully ahead into the one so newly begun. Then, all very tired, we sensibly decided that the wisest thing would be to make our way back to our beds. Before doing this, we prayed quietly together, then standing, we pulled on our macs. As we struggled into our still damp things, the electric lights went out completely and did not flicker on again. In the candlelight the wind sounded more alarming than ever, hissing and throwing itself vehemently against the large windows.

'Hi, look at the windows on the west side of the room, the glass is actually moving,' cried Pat in alarm. 'Say, I really hoped I'd get to see a gale whilst I was over here, though this is going a bit far!'

We laughed at her as we slipped into our gumboots. 'Even I, after nearly eight years in Shetland, can't boast of a wind like this,' I said, giving a final tug to my boot. 'Come on, let's get out and face it. Sister Mary Clare and I will see you two into your chalets before we go up to The Ness.'

Lamps blown out and the workshop door well secured, we walked relatively easily along the side of the building, saying goodnight to the two of them at their own doors. Then, stepping out into the main thrust of the wind, we two Sisters, clinging tightly together, bent double so that we could see only a pool of waving torchlight at our feet, were blown up the hardcore road at a considerable speed. The wind was behind us and coming off the sea, which was, we later decided, a great blessing.

Reaching home we wasted no time in going to our rooms, where we were soon warm and snug despite the fact that the noise of the storm was, we thought, going to make it impossible to sleep. I wondered if The Ness would stand the strain, for it sounded as though the windows were not only shaking but about to fall in. Pulling the duvet over my head I said a few extra prayers and yes, surprisingly, I did sleep.

When Frances arrived the next morning for Terce, all was calm, though she breezed in with some tempestuous news. Not only had her caravan been pushed further over than it already was, but now Rosemary's caravan had gone over too. We dashed out to look and there, in a corner of Lower Ness garden, was a battered heap of what had been the sturdy and cosy little caravan that Rosemary had made so much use of during the summers. We could hardly believe our eyes for, like Greenbank, it had been roped down firmly and staked into the ground. As it was, the stakes had been wrenched out, the caravan lifted about thirty feet from its original position and then the whole thing dashed down and smashed. Yes . . . Pat had seen a storm and a half.

Poor Rosemary was in bed with the flu at the time and was too ill to cope with any thoughts of her wrecked 'bolt hole'. So later that morning I gave Kenny a ring and he and Robert, his son-in-law, (for my friend Anne is now married) came along and roped the wreckage down to the ground to prevent any further dangerous blowing around. The rest of us picked up Rosemary's sodden books lying around the garden and salvaged what we could from the remains of the caravan.

Our homes, fortunately, were unscathed, apart from two tiles that had loosened on the roof of Tigh Sith. For this escape, we counted ourselves most blessed, especially when we heard that the wind speed of that New Year gale was recorded on the Island of Unst, four miles north of Fetlar, at 212 miles per hour! Many Shetland homes were damaged, two young people were killed and a whole caravan site on the Shetland Mainland wiped out.

A few days into the New Year, Kerry returned home, leaving Pat to stay on a short while longer. We thoroughly enjoyed having them both and by the time Pat's visit came to an end, we were talking seriously of her return. The four of us felt strongly that God was asking her to come to Fetlar and join forces with us as a member of the community, though in what capacity within our group we cannot tell, until her call has been tested. After that, we shall be shown exactly if and where she is meant to fit in.

For we are indeed as St Peter said, 'living stones', of varying shapes and sizes, and can only be fitted together by the great Master Builder Himself.[1] If Shetland stones are anything to go by, then for each of us it will take a while to be found our own special niche – a niche where somewhere, within the construction, we can remain unmoved whatever storms of life hit us. It seems to me that the Lord, like every wall builder I know, tries and tests each stone in a particular place and often in several places. With Rose, for example, perhaps he has tried, tested and lifted her down again and is waiting patiently until the right cavity for her own exact and unique shape will appear. The rest of us seem to be a right fit at the first try, as far as SOLI is concerned, though I expect in the future the Lord will try many others who are only in passing.

Pat is courageous and has, as I have already said, a lovely sense of humour. This week she will be returning to her own country where she is determined to wind up her affairs and return as soon as she can, which we hope will be in the summer of this year 1992.

What else this year holds for us we do not know, for our story has caught up with me. We have finally decided that we shall not be pushing ahead with the building project, for we need a pause; a month or two to stand back and take stock, and also take in a deep breath after all the hard work of Phase One. Whether we shall have taken up the threads again and will be making plans to erect our own simple home and chapel by this time next year remains to be seen. We like to think that we might be, for it will make life so much simpler when we are down on the headland. However, a great deal of money has still to be raised even for the most basic of buildings. This is partly, of course, because we believe that we are being asked to do it on a remote northerly isle. All we can ever do, certainly at this stage, is to offer ourselves, our whole selves, body, mind and soul, to God and leave the timing to him. It is easy to become impatient – but patience is all part of the course. God's timing is perfect. Ours is not.

Pat's holiday has come to an end; a few days ago Sister Mary Clare and I brought her to see Da Gaets and took her over to Walls to visit the registrar there. We hoped that he could throw a little more light on the subject of her mother's side of the family. When at last we tracked him down, much to her delight his information proved very helpful.

It was fun having time with her in our little hermitage and away from our day-by-day work at home on Fetlar. For here we had an opportunity to spend time with her and see lovely glimpses of a very dear and deep-thinking person. It also gave her a chance to see another side, perhaps a less pressured side, of us. Yesterday we took her into Lerwick and with mixed emotions said our au revoirs.

Now we're back at Da Gaets for another day, though we have already turned our faces towards Fetlar. It is beneficial to step aside, yet always we are conscious that there, over the layers of hills and stretches of sea, lies home . . . Yes, our hearts warm at the thought. Sister Mary Clare is longing to get back to her golden goat and her craft work, and I to Skerry, Flugga, Mooskit and my word processor – and of course, to our faithful friends holding the fort whilst we are away.

We load the car with our bedding, then go back and forth loading other oddments, such as the picnic basket containing the necessary flask and bite to eat on the ferries.

With the house door locked we stand and take a last loving look at our special hermitage place. Taking Sister Mary Clare's hand, for I'm no longer afraid of touch, I listen. The lark has not returned, yet we can hear her song . . . We neither stir nor speak . . . there is no need . . . We know that what we hear is the song of our hearts, the song of love, and that in it we have the same gifts of joy and freedom as our friend the lark . . . We know that there's no need of fear with regard to anything that life holds for us. For despite our vulnerability we are bound to our Creator and in our binding, we are free.

> Hail to thee, blithe Spirit!
>   Bird thou never wert,
> That from Heaven, or near it,
>   Pourest thy full heart
> In profuse strains of unpremeditated art.[2]

A sudden soft wind caresses our cheeks . . . a faint promise of spring is in the air. We climb into the car and turn for home . . .

Words of the Shetland poet George P.S. Peterson from Papa Stour come to me as we wind up the valley.

> 'Tell me – peerie laeverick – tell me
>   Sallen du come back agyen?'
> 'Yea, ye'll hear me i da voar days
>   Singing trow da wind and rain.'

'Wha will guide de, peerie laeverick –
    Guide de ower da ragin sea?'
'Him at bids is just ta trust Him –
    Him at made baith me and de.'[3]

'Tell me – tiny lark bird – tell me
    Will you not come back again?'
'Yes, you'll hear me in the spring time
    Singing through the wind and rain.'

'Who will guide you, tiny larkbird –
    Guide you o'er the raging sea?'
'He who bids us just to trust Him –
    He that made both me and thee.'

And, as we came to The Ness some hours later, I said, 'I know, let's
call our new home, when we manage to build it, "Larks' Hame".'

Notes

Prologue
1 C. Day Lewis (1904-72), two stanzas of 'The Ecstatic' from *The Complete Poems of C. Day Lewis*, ed. Jill Balcon (Sinclair-Stevenson 1992) © The Estate of C. Day Lewis.

Chapter 2 FLEDGELINGS
1 Angelus Silesius (1624-77), 'The Spiritual Maxims', from *Perfection of Love*, ed. Tony Castle (Fount 1986).

Chapter 3 FLUTTER OF WINGS
1 A Celtic prayer, from *The Carmina Gadelica* (Scottish Academic Press).
2 Isaiah 35.1, RV.

Chapter 4 DARK WINGED SKY
1 A quote from *The Carmina Gadelica*.
2 2 Corinthians 4.6 KJV
3 A Celtic prayer, from *The Celtic Vision*.

Chapter 5 RETURN TO THE NEST
1 Angelus Silesius, 'Rhymes of a German Mystic', from *The Perfection of Love*.

Chapter 6 FLYING INTO THE WIND
1 Angelus Silesius, 'The Spiritual Maxims', from *The Perfection of Love*.

Chapter 8 WHEELS OF FLIGHT
1 *Veni Creator Spiritus*, trans. Robert Bridges (1844–1930) in *The English Hymnal* (Oxford University Press 1906) 154.
2 David Adam, 'Love Remains Eternally', from *Tides and Seasons* (Triangle 1989).

Chapter 9 FEATHER FRAIL
1 Based on Ephesians 6.13–18.
2 Luke 12.22 KJV.
3 Luke 12.23–24 KJV.
4 Philippians 4.4, 5 KJV.

Chapter 10 WAFTED WESTWARDS
1 Antiphon to the Magnificat, Good Shepherd Sunday, from *The Divine Office* (Society of St Margaret, East Grinstead, published by Oxford University Press 1953).

Chapter 11 RISE TO THE CLOUDS
1 Isaiah 12.13 KJV.
2 Versicle and Response for the feast of Our Lady of Joy, from *The Divine Office*.

Chapter 12 WINGS OF LOVE
1 1 Peter 2.5 KJV
2 A Celtic prayer, from *The Carmina Gadelica*.

Chapter 13 FLIGHT PATTERNS
1 A Celtic prayer; from *The Carmina Gadelica*

Chapter 15 FREEDOM'S PINIONS
1 Angelus Silesius, 'Rhymes of a German Mystic', from *The Perfection of Love*.

Chapter 16 WIDENING CIRCLES
1 Bishop John Cosin (1594–1672), based on *Veni, Creator Spiritus, English Hymnal* 153.

Chapter 17 A MIGRANT
1 1 Peter 2.5.
2 Percy Bysshe Shelley (1792–1822), 'Ode to a Skylark'.
3 From *Da dee up, du's welcome!* by Stella Shepherd and George Peterson.